Thanks for Your trust!

One of the best ways to educate children is entertain them at the same time.

In this book, You can find lots of mazes and exercises to improve handwriting skills.

Activities such as coloring will improve your child's pencil grip, as well as helping them to relax, self regulate their mood and develop their imagination.

Moreover they will improve hand – eye coordination.

We wish You great time with our activity book!

We will be glad if You will get us a comment.

Index

THEORY

Introduction

The concepts of dyslexia, dysgraphia, dysorthography, or specific difficulties in learning to read and write are widely described on the subject's literature. Multiple specialists are concerned with the problem of developmental dyslexia.

Developmental dyslexia is a disorder that cannot be outgrown or cured. People who faces this problem are burdened with it for the rest of their lives. Depending on its severity, there are various difficulties and consequences later in life.

Specific difficulties in learning to read and write are in generally speaking problems in acquiring the skills of recognizing letters, analysis and voice synthesis, and mess in learning to read. It is also closely related to writing – the child makes numerous spelling and inflected mistakes. Moreover, there is an unsightly handwriting, the letters are shapeless, the words do not fit in the lines, which makes the notes chaotic and difficult to read.

Terminology

The term 'Specific Learning Difficulty' (SpLD) is a term that refers to a difference or difficulty with particular aspects of learning. The most common SpLDs are dyslexia, dyspraxia, attention deficit-hyperactivity disorder, dyscalculia and dysgraphia. An individual may have one of these independently or they can co-exist as part of a wider profile.Specific Learning Difficulties (SpLDs) exist on a continuum from mild to moderate through to severe. There are common patterns of behaviour and ability, but there will be a range of different patterns of effects for each individual.

Working methods

The problem of dyslexia is a persistent and non-periodic phenomenon, which is why it often affects a person's entire life. A very important role is played by the psychological and pedagogical diagnosis as well as the cooperation of various entities in order to best help the child. Helena Grzelachowska puts the family in the first place, which should carefully observe the child from the moment of birth, under the guidance of a pediatrician and psychologist.

The role of parents is to support the child and to surround him with unconditional love, thanks to which it will allow the child to reduce the level of anxiety and frustration, and this will make him able to achieve success. Educational institutions play an important role. Already in the kindergarten and even in the nursery, educators may notice developmental abnormalities that indicate that the child is at the "risk of dyslexia". The task of teachers at school is to take into account the needs of children with specific learning difficulties through the use of appropriate teaching methods.

The main advanteges of exercises:

- develop to dexterity

- develop hand - eye coordination

- improve patient

- improvement of perceptiveness

- develop memory

- stimulation of imagination

- improve counting skills

- stimulation of brain

- provide to fun.

Handwriting exercises

Let's Start warming Up:

O

Trace the Number 0

Zero

Trace the word Zero

1

Trace the Number 1

One

Trace the word One

One One One One
One One One One
One One One One
One One One One

1

One

Write Number 1

1
1
1
1

Color One Orange

Trace the Number 2

2

Trace the word Two

Two

Write Number 2

2
2
2
2

Color Two Apples

Two

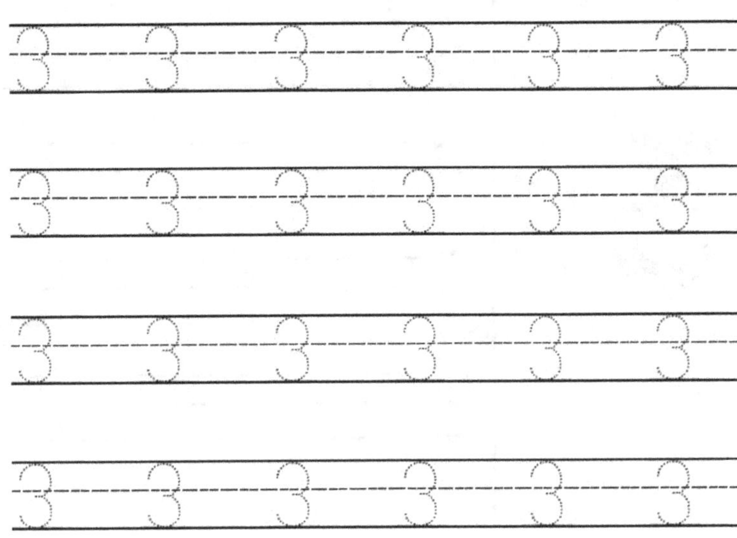

Trace the Number 3

Trace the word Three

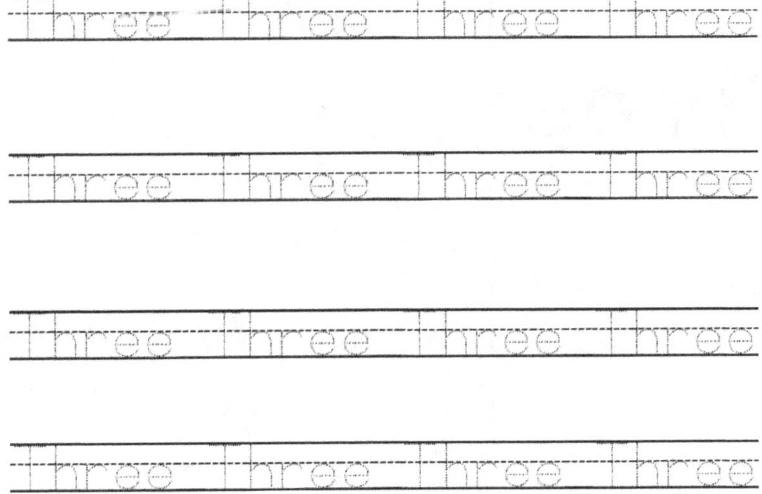

Write Number 3

3

3
3
3
3

Color Three Pears

Three

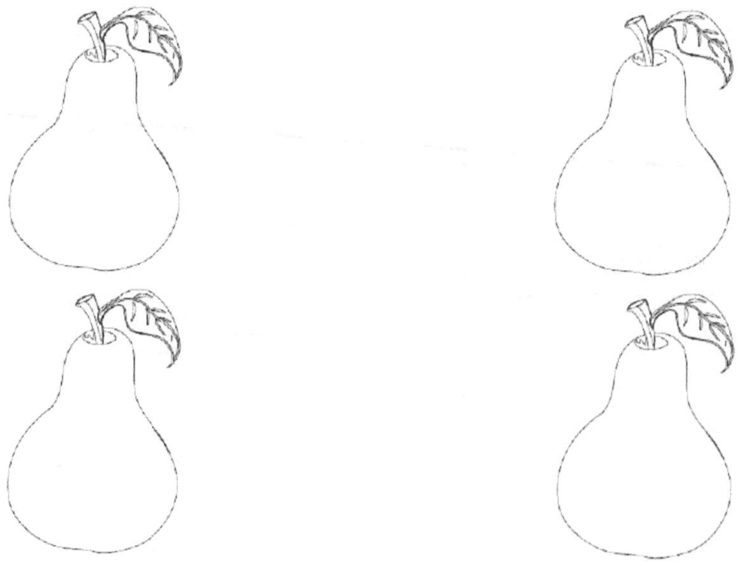

4

Trace the Number 4

Four

Trace the word Four

4

Write Number 4

4 4 4 4

Four

Color Four water Melon slices

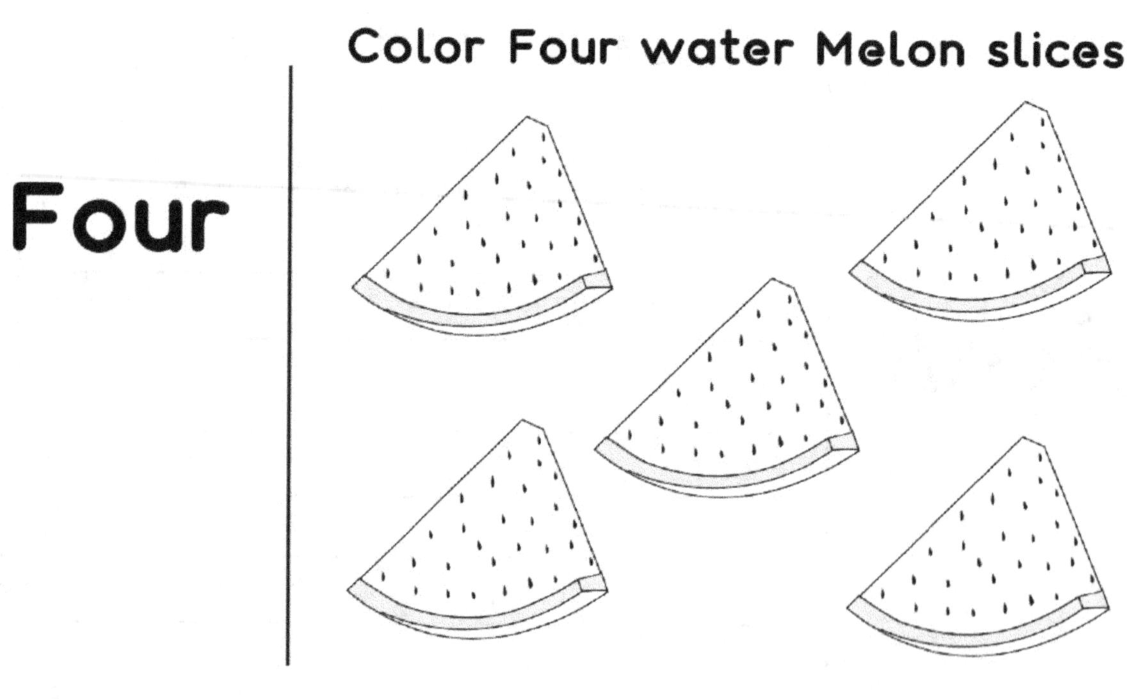

5

Trace the Number 5

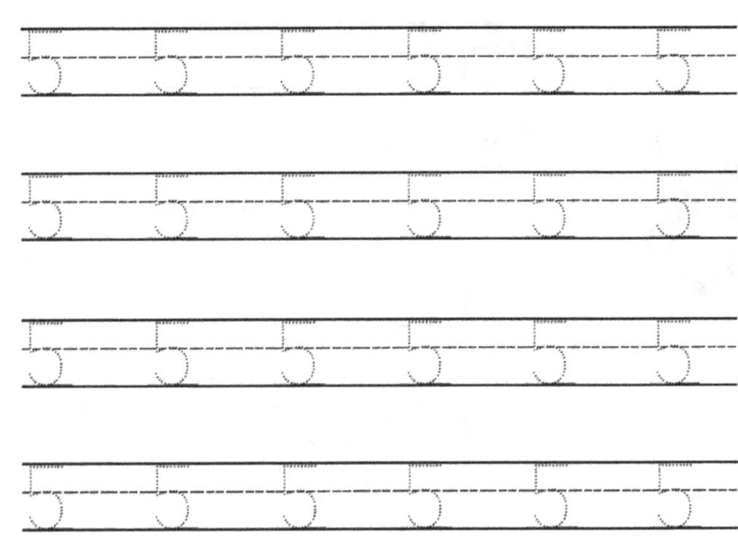

Five

Trace the word Five

Write Number 5

5

5
5
5
5

Color Five Tomatoes

Five

6

Trace the Number 6

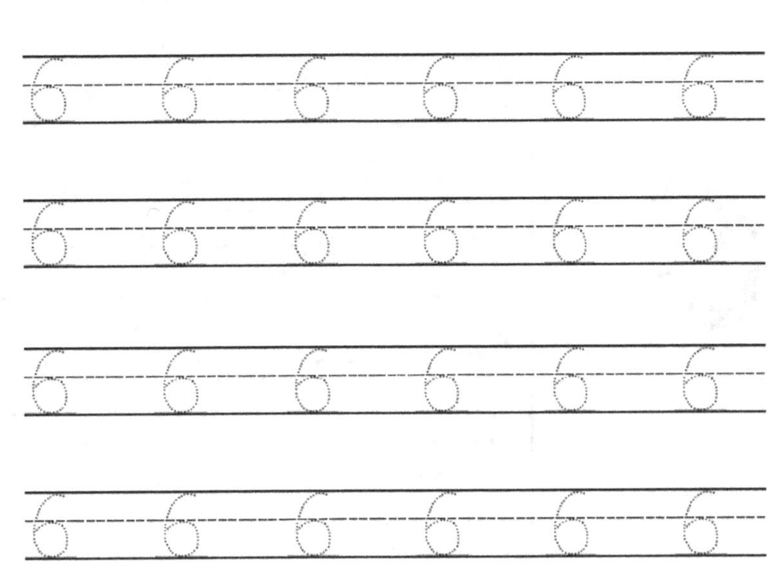

Six

Trace the word Six

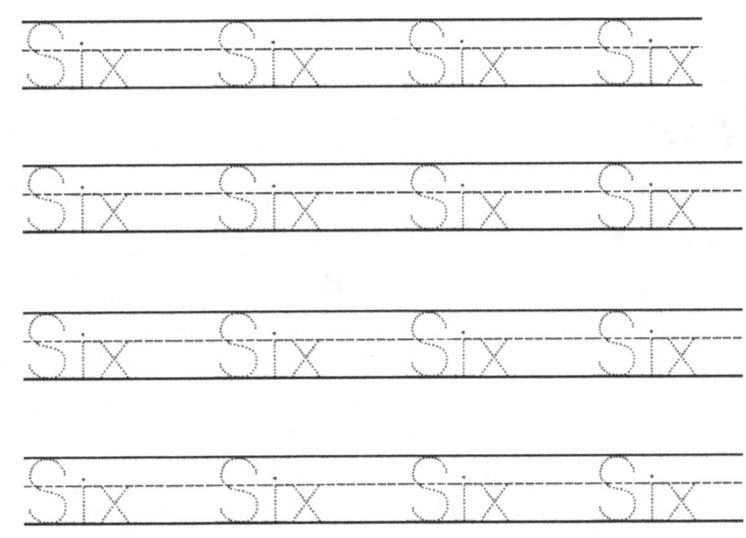

6

Write Number 6

6
6
6
6

Six

Color Six Carrots

Trace the Number 7

Trace the word Seven

7

Seven

Write Number 7

7
7
7
7

7

Seven

Color Seven Pumpkins

Trace the Number 8

8

Trace the word Eight

Eight

Write Number 8

8

8

8

8

8

Eight

Color Eight Strawberries

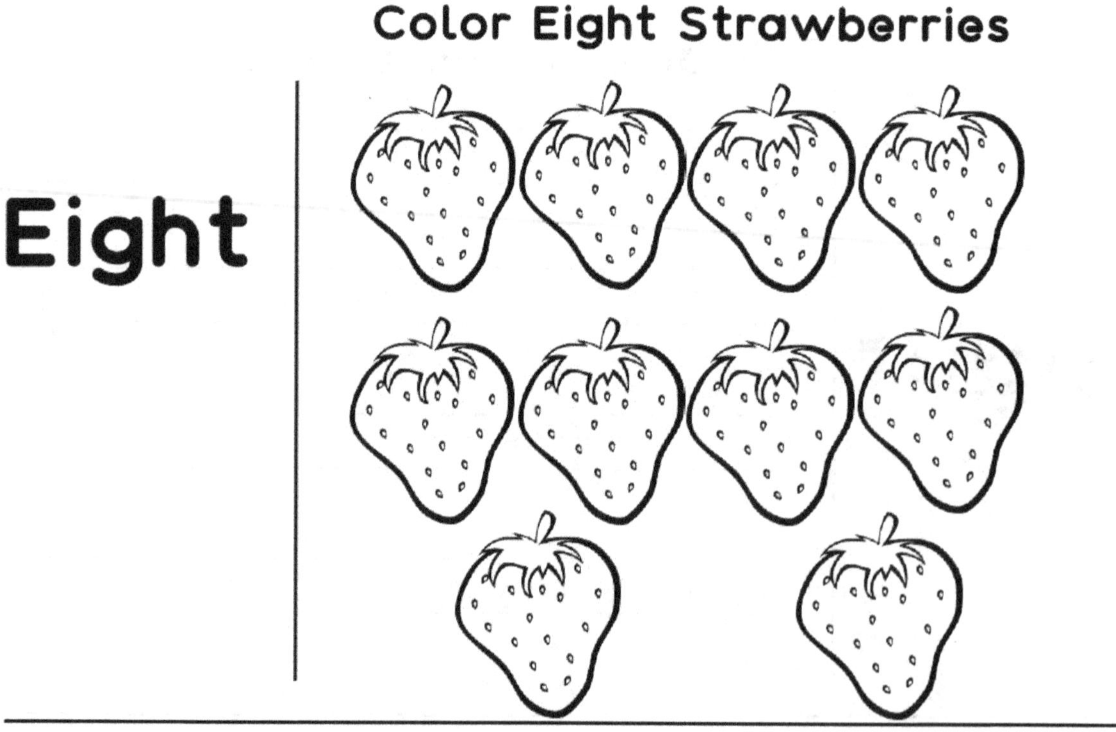

Trace the Number 9

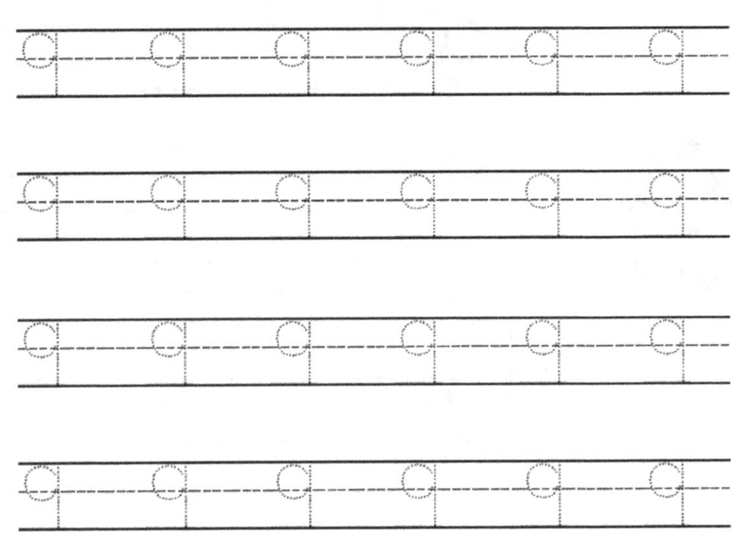

Trace the word Nine

Write Number 9

9 9 9 9

9

Color nine Spikes of wheat

Nine

Trace the Number 10

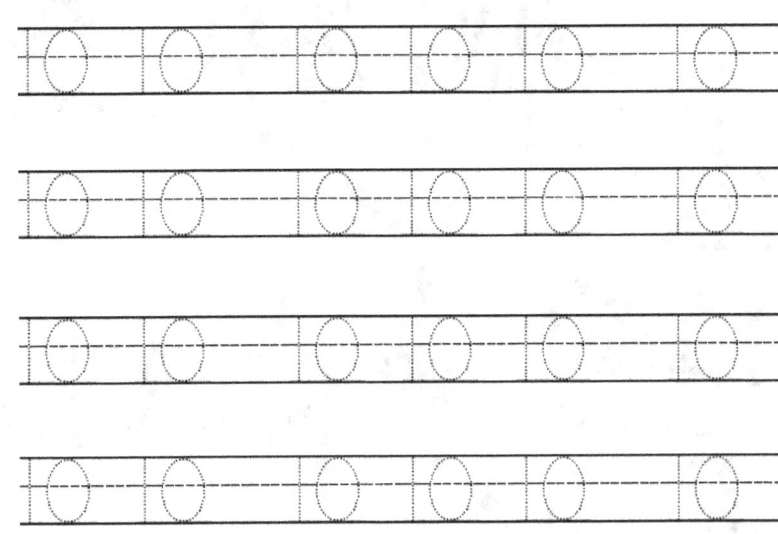

10

Trace the word Ten

Ten

Dot
to
dots

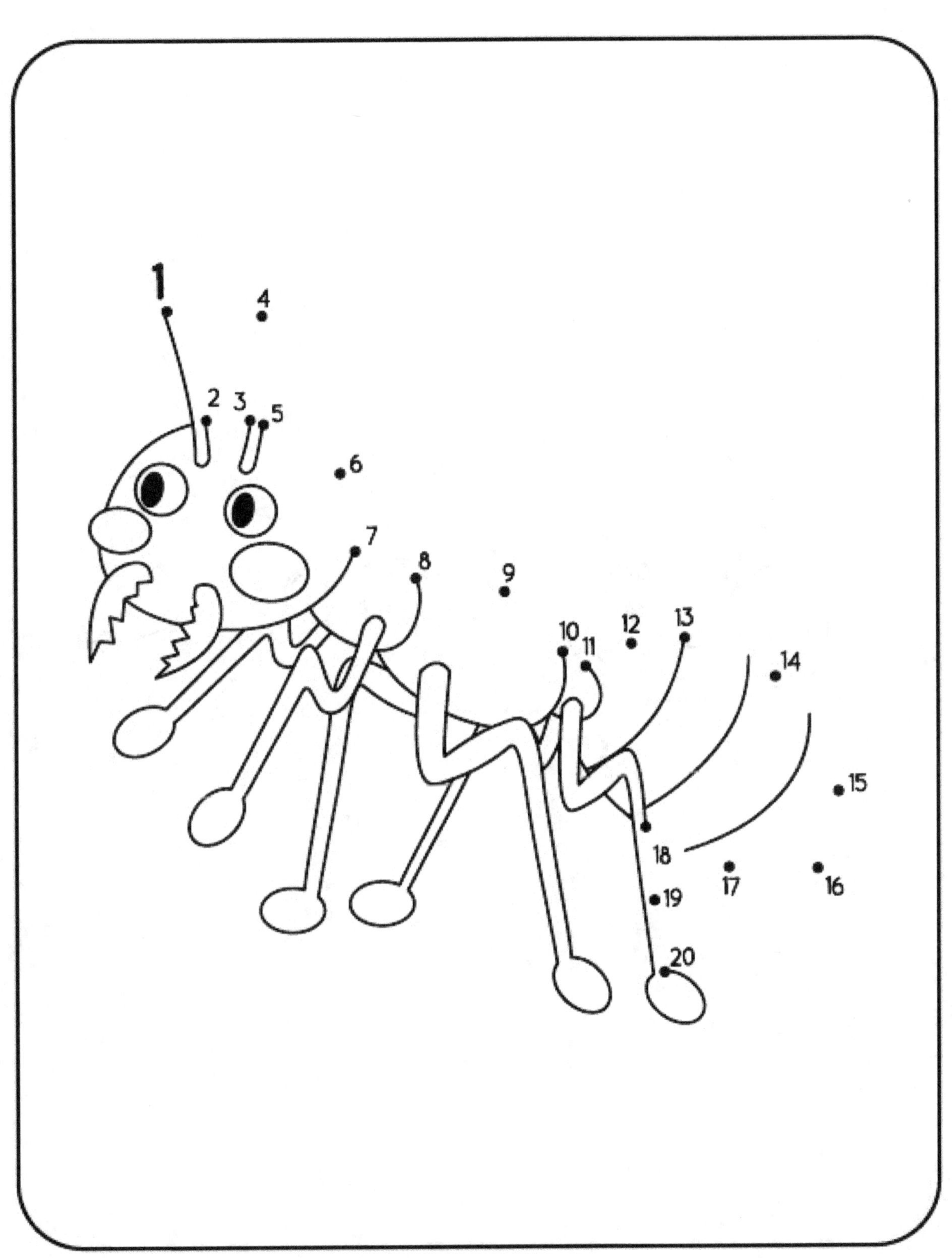1
4
2 3 5
6
7
8
9
10 11 12 13
14
15
18
17 16
19
20

1
2
3
4
5
6
7
8
9
10

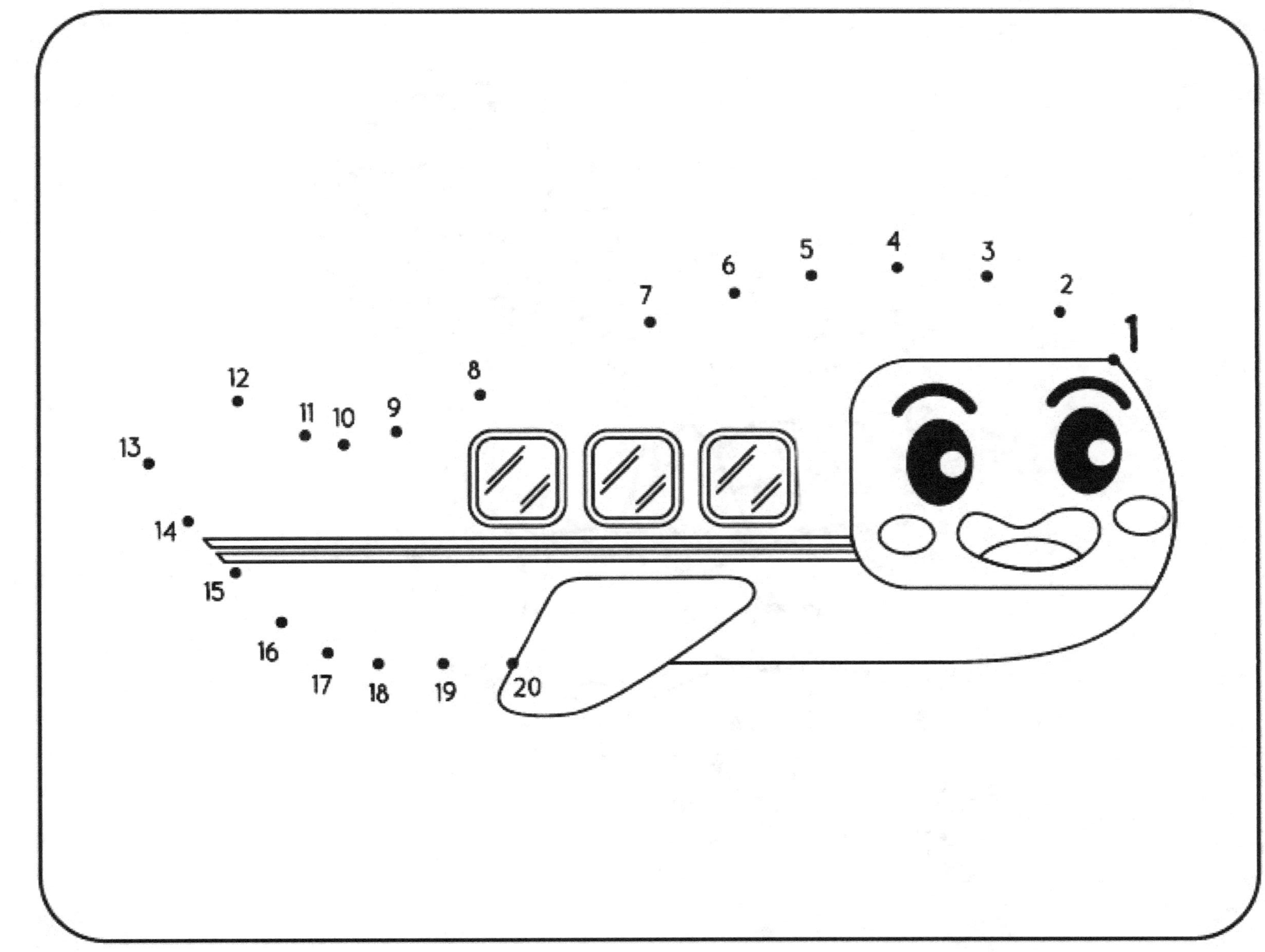

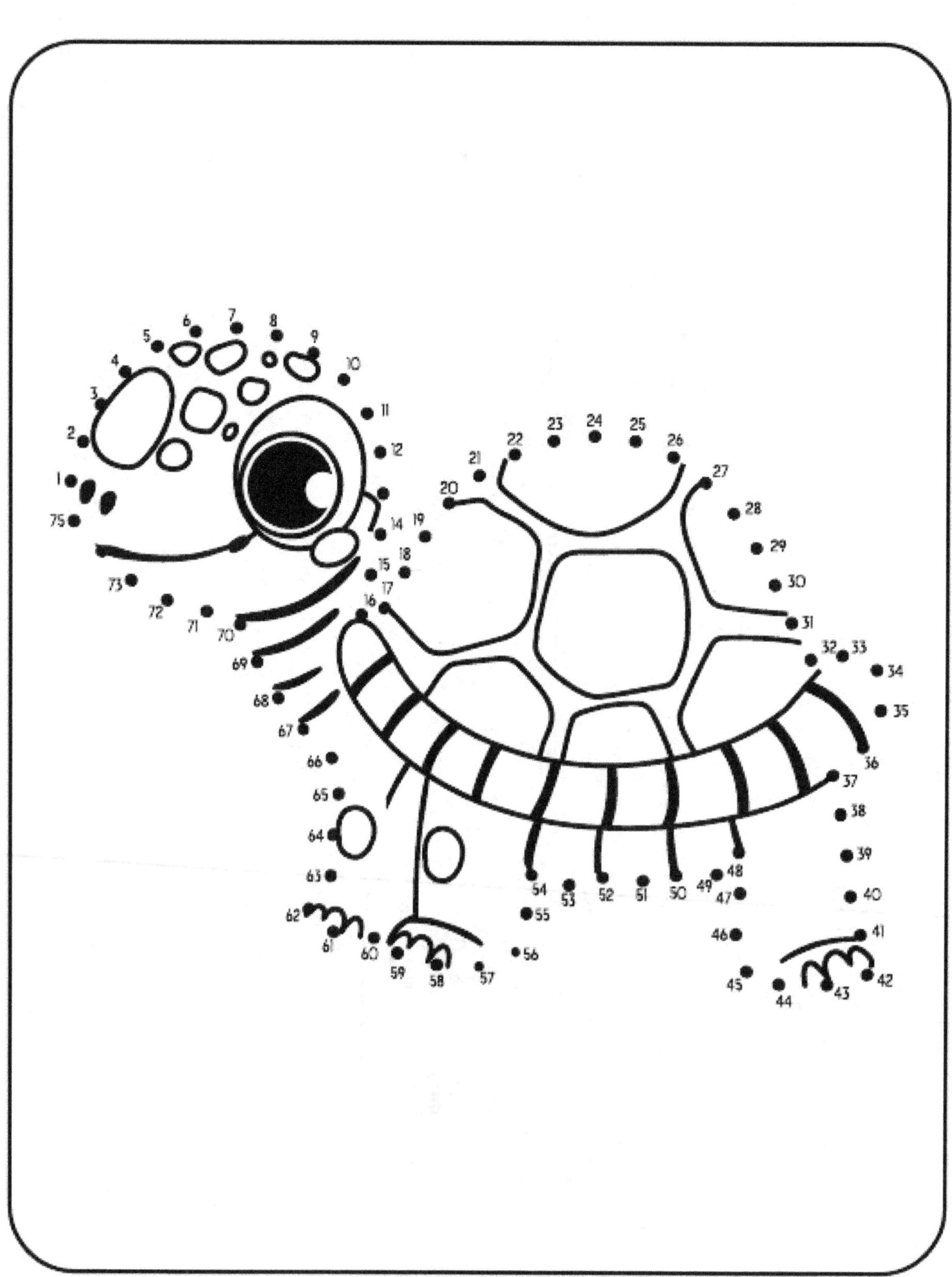

1
33
2
32
31
30
3
29
5
4
28
6
27
26
7
25
8
24
9
23
10
11
22
21
20
12
19
13
14
15
16
17
18

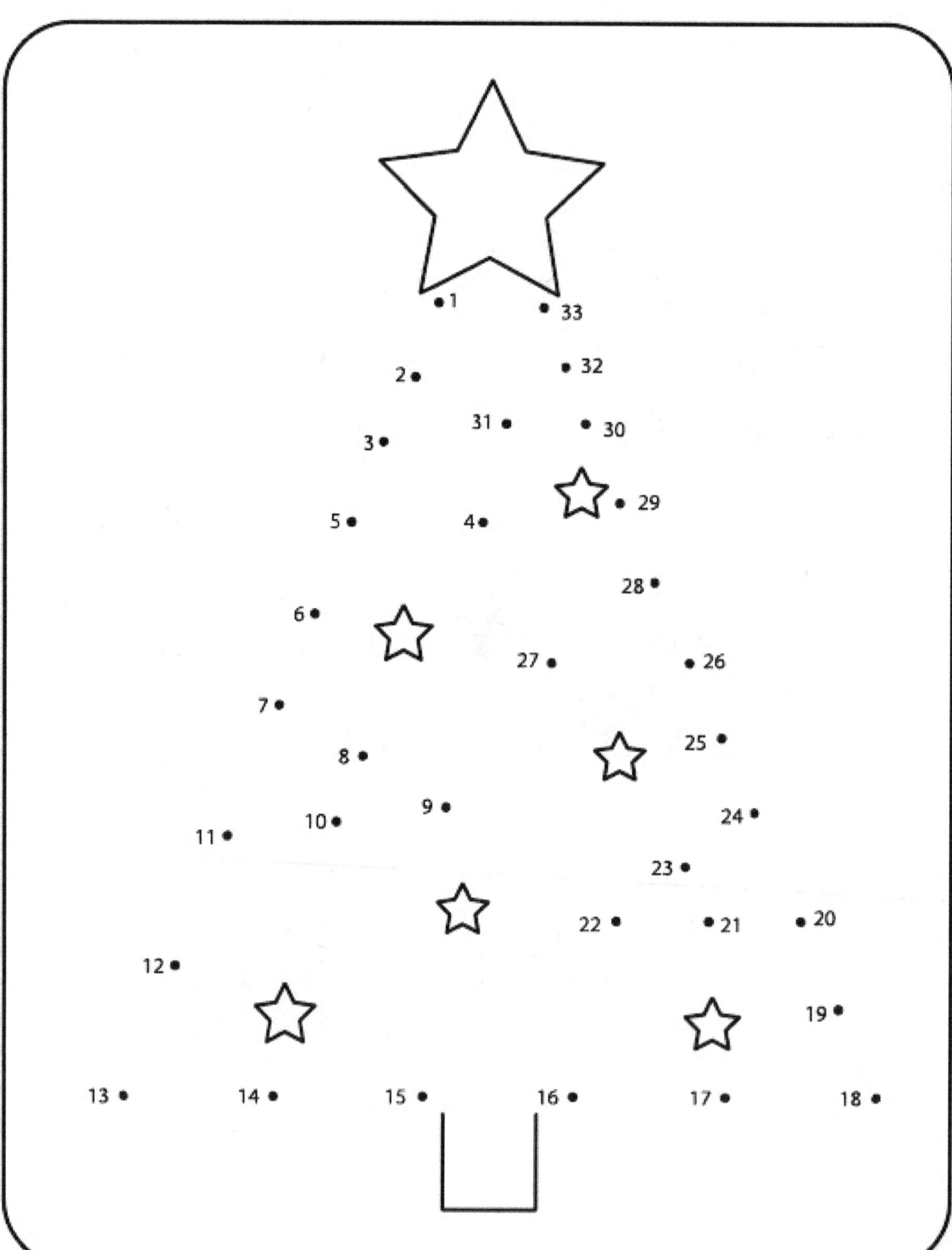

38

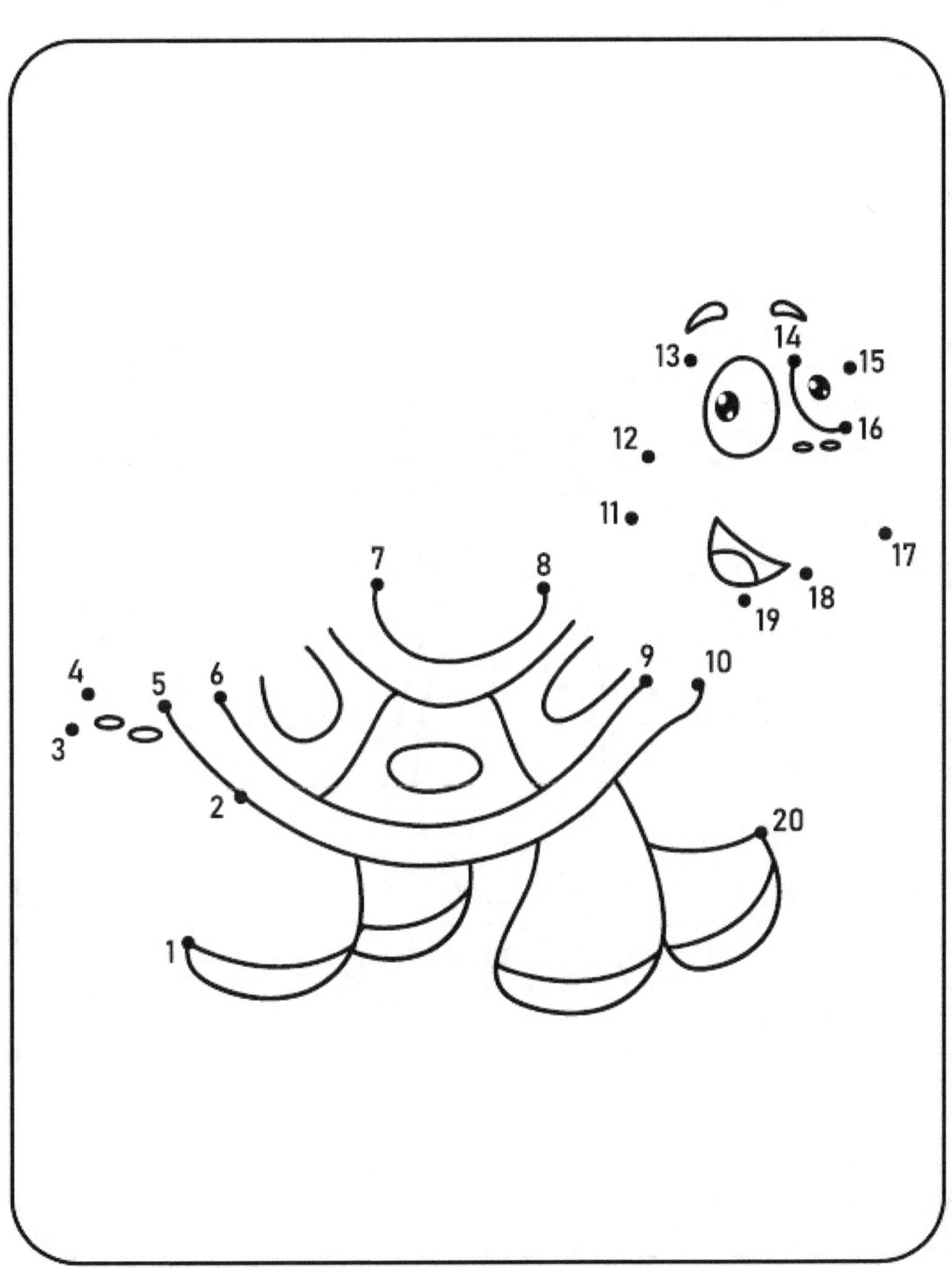

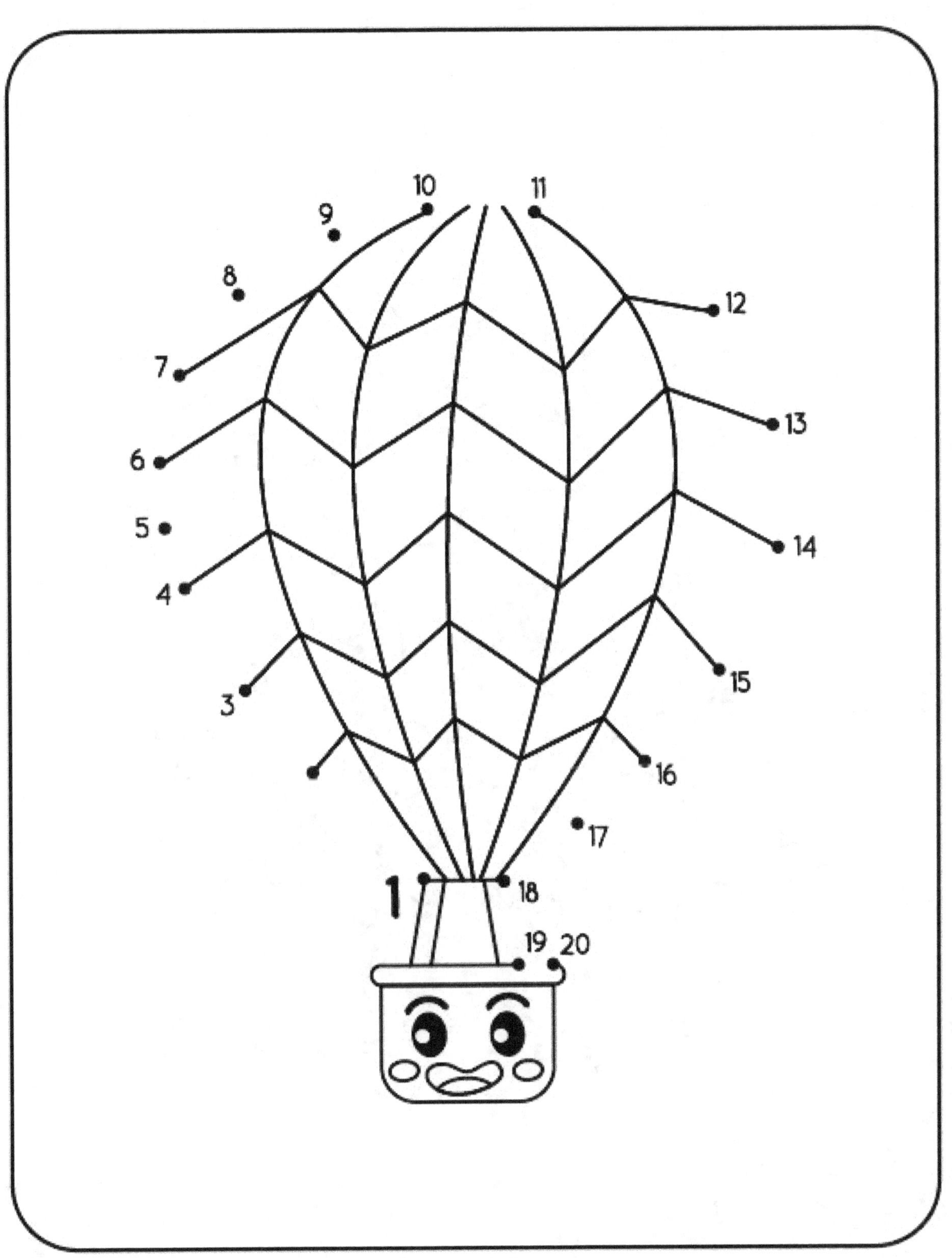

1
3
4
5
6
7
8
9
10
11
12
13
14
15
16
17
18
19
20

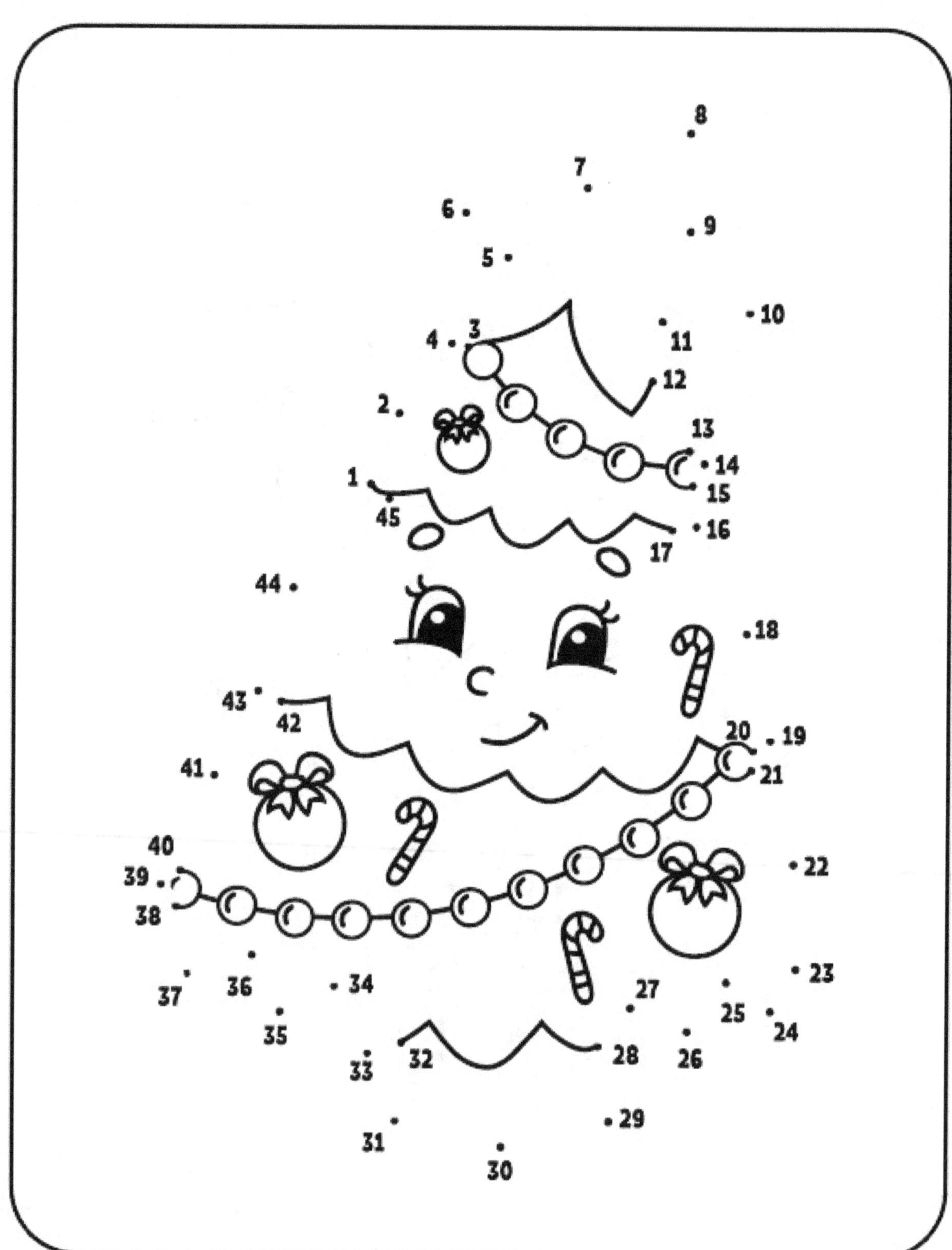

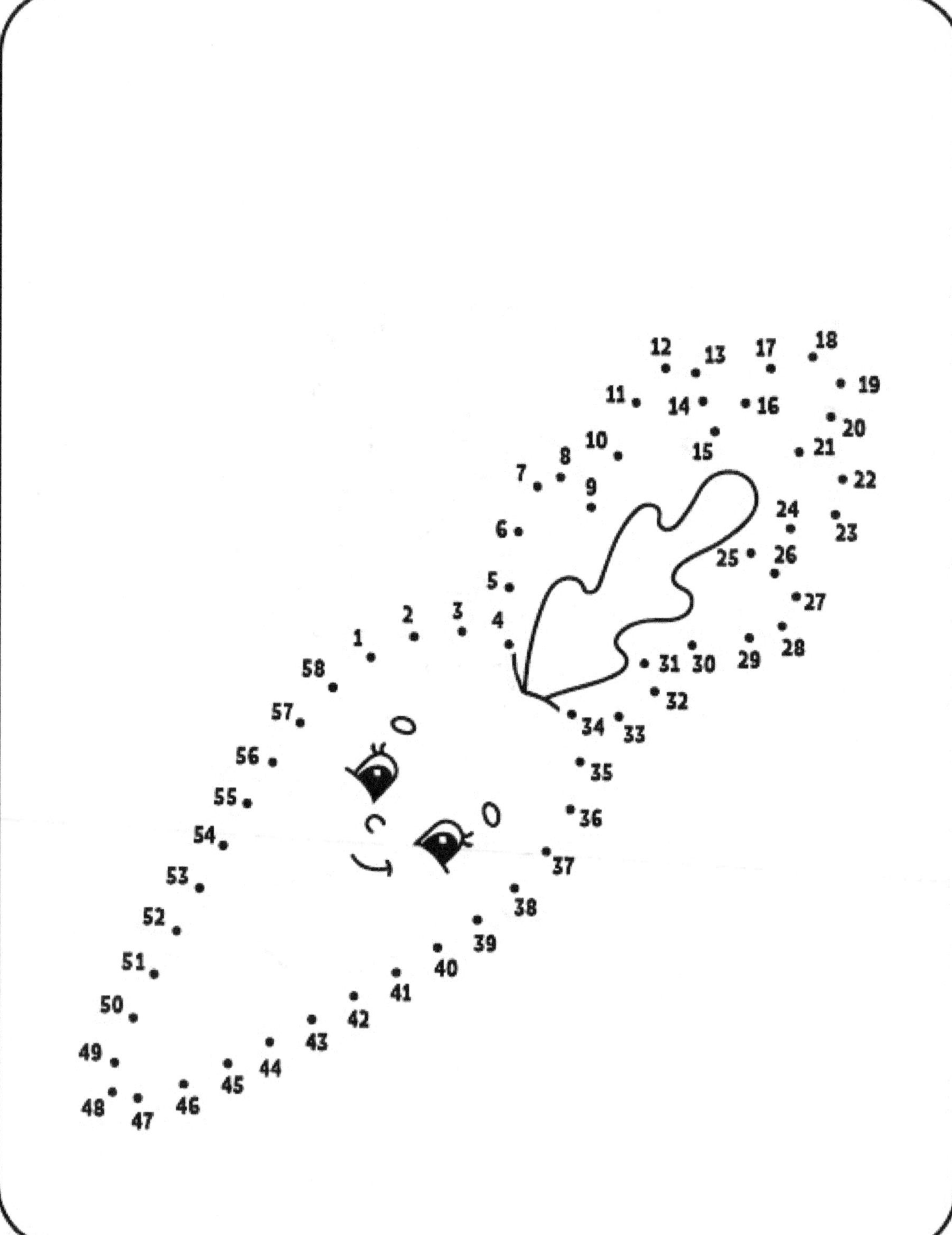

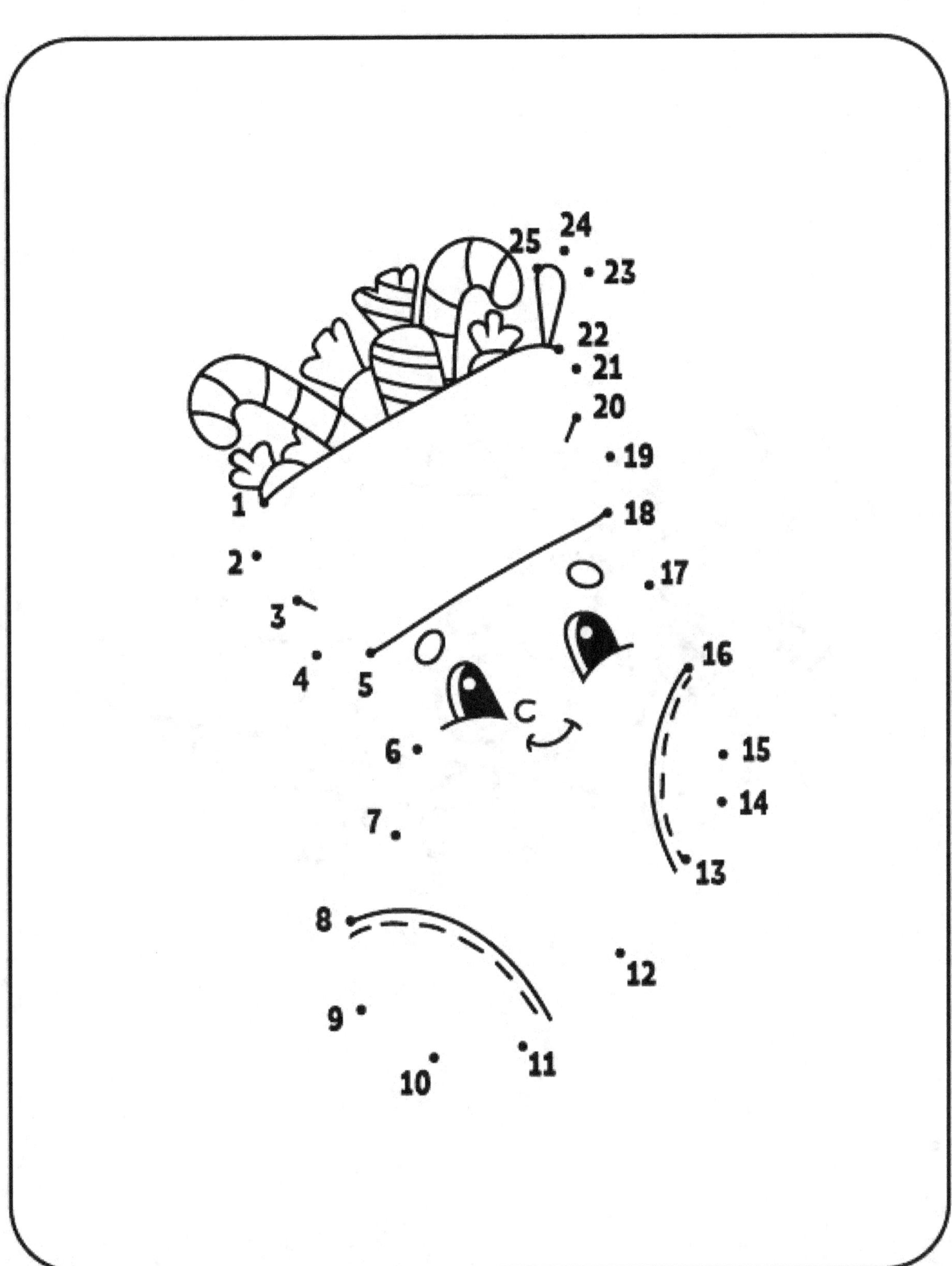

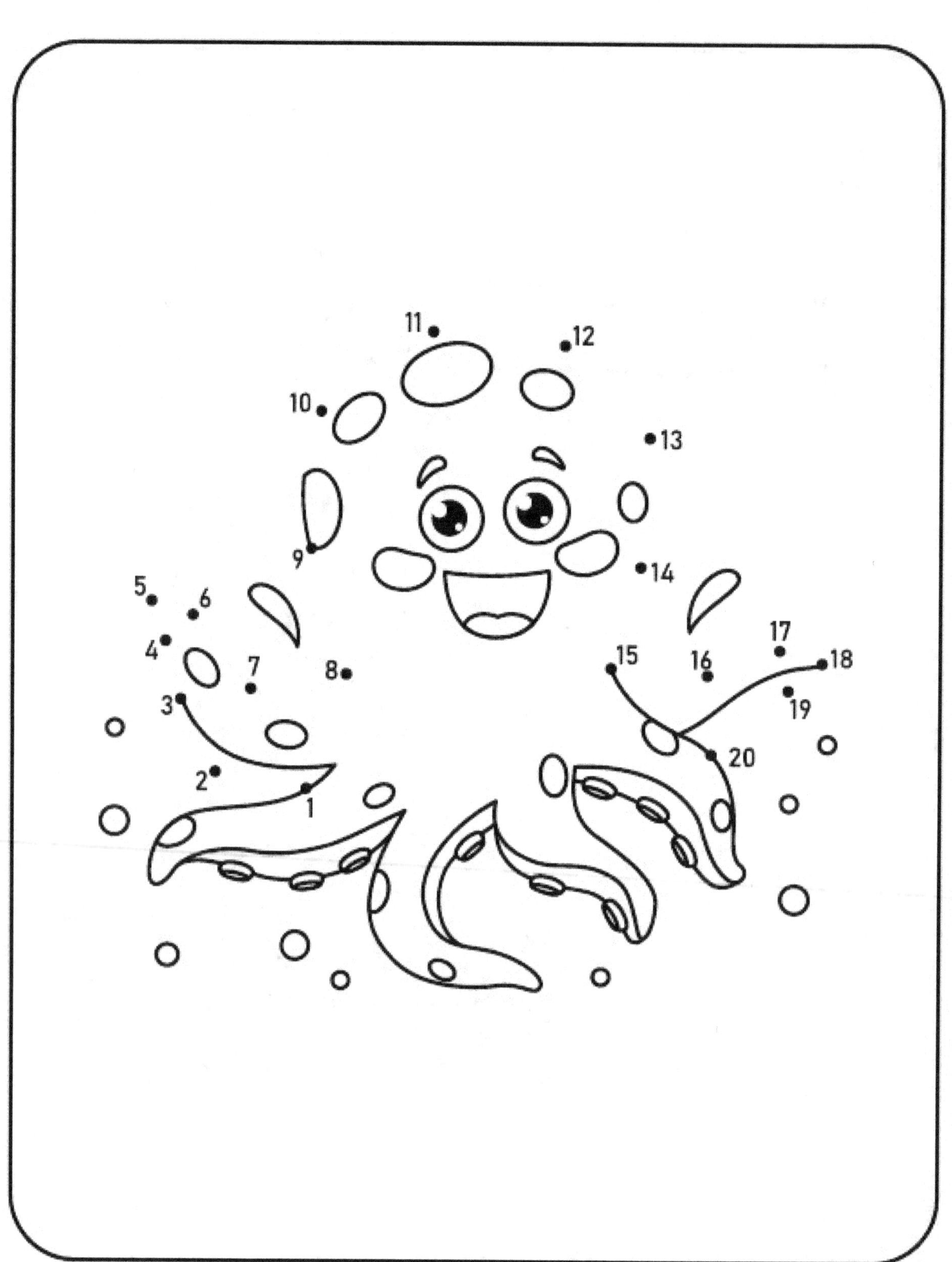

10
1
9
2
8
3
7
4
6
5

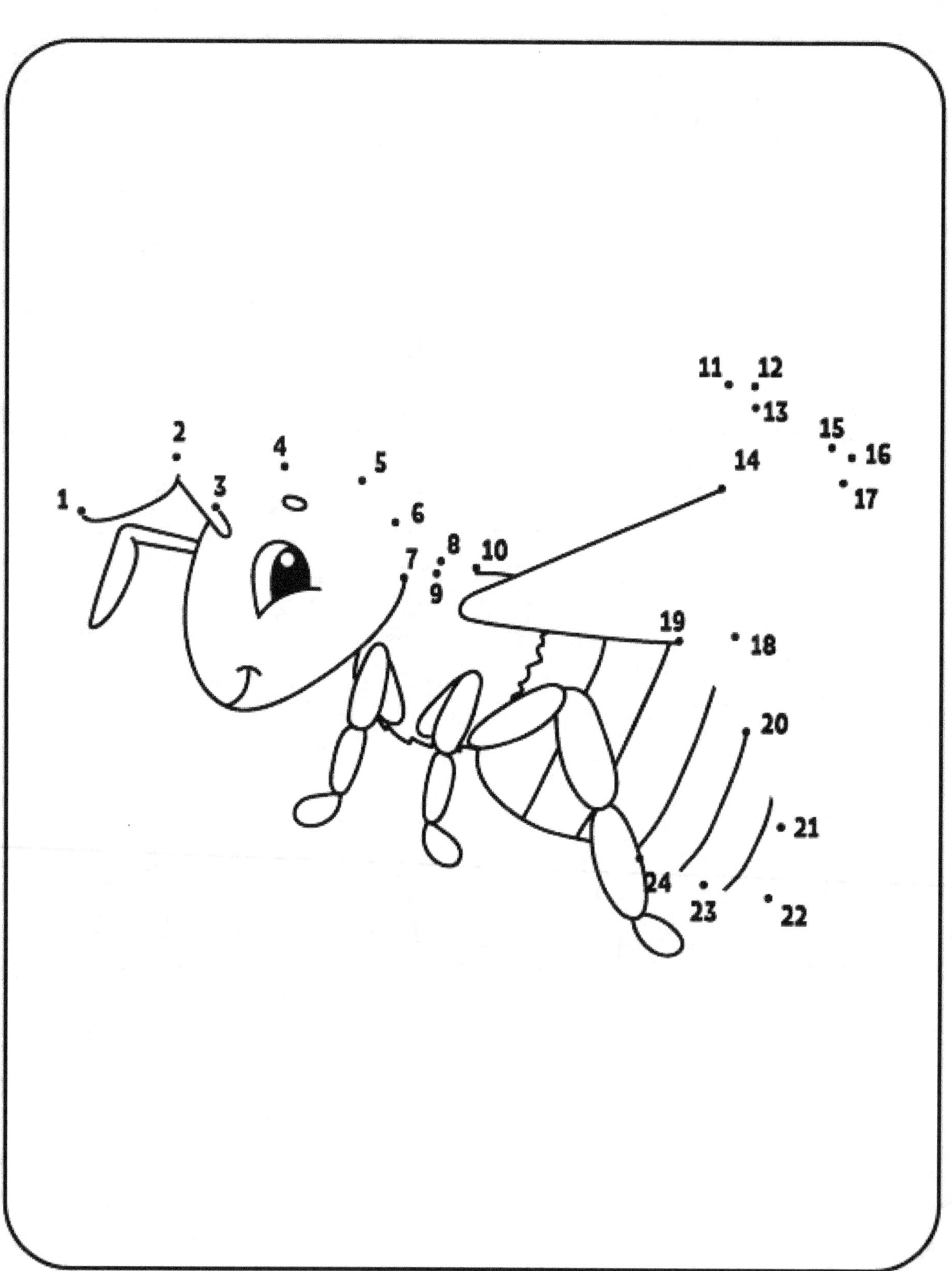

1
2
3
4
5
6
7
8
9
10
11
12
13
14
15
16
17
18
19
20
21
22
23
24

Mazes

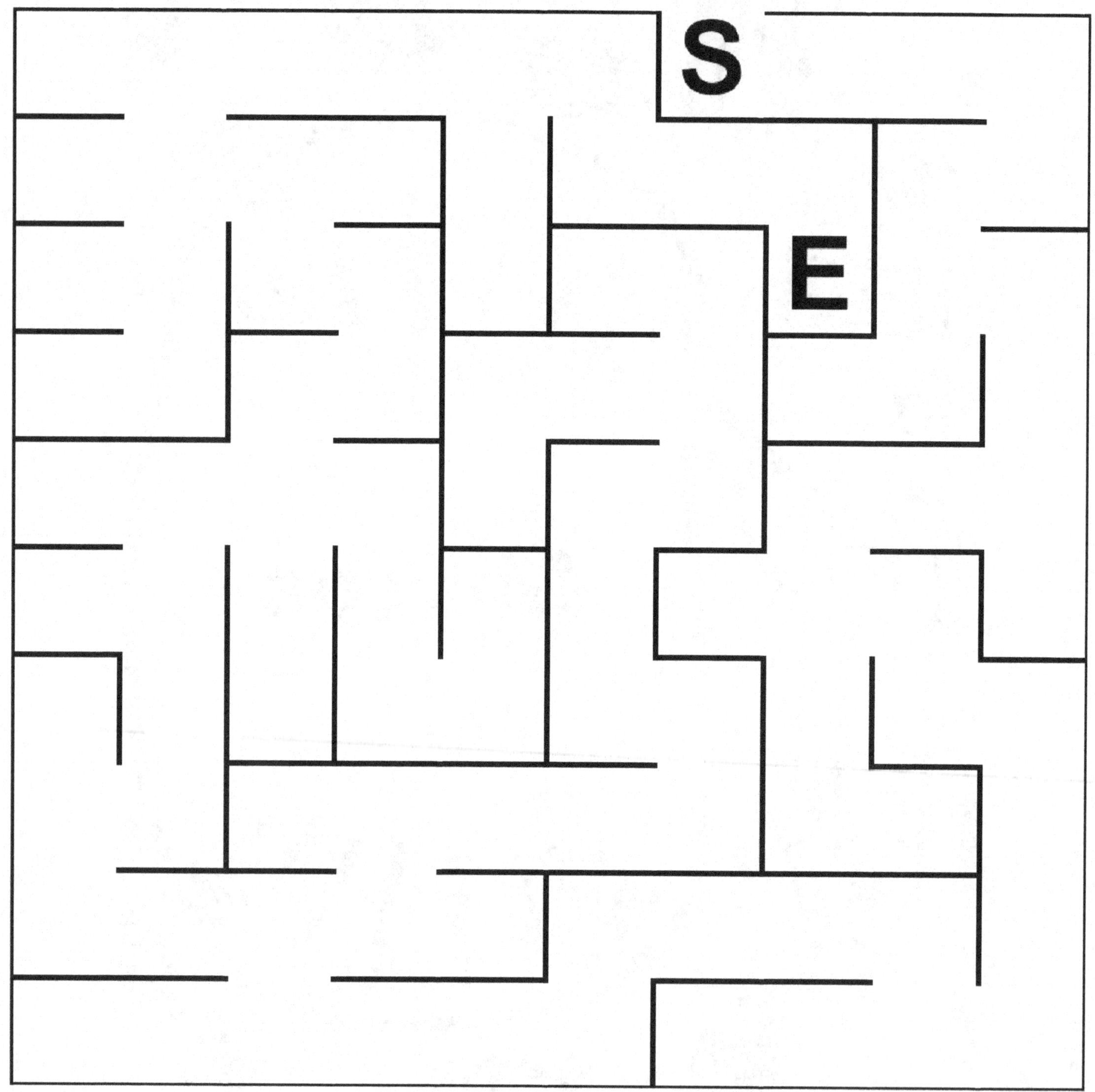

S
E

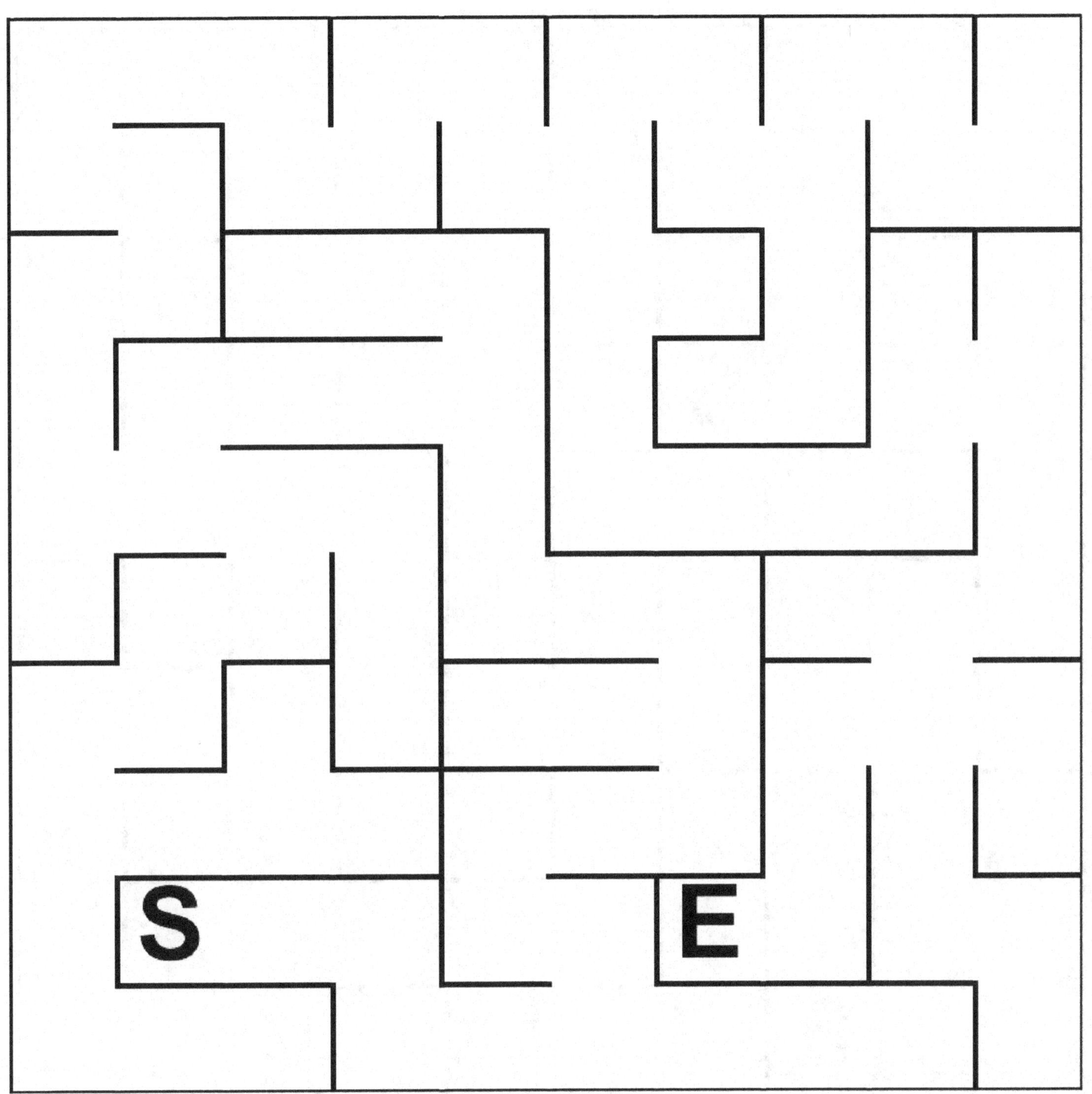

S
E

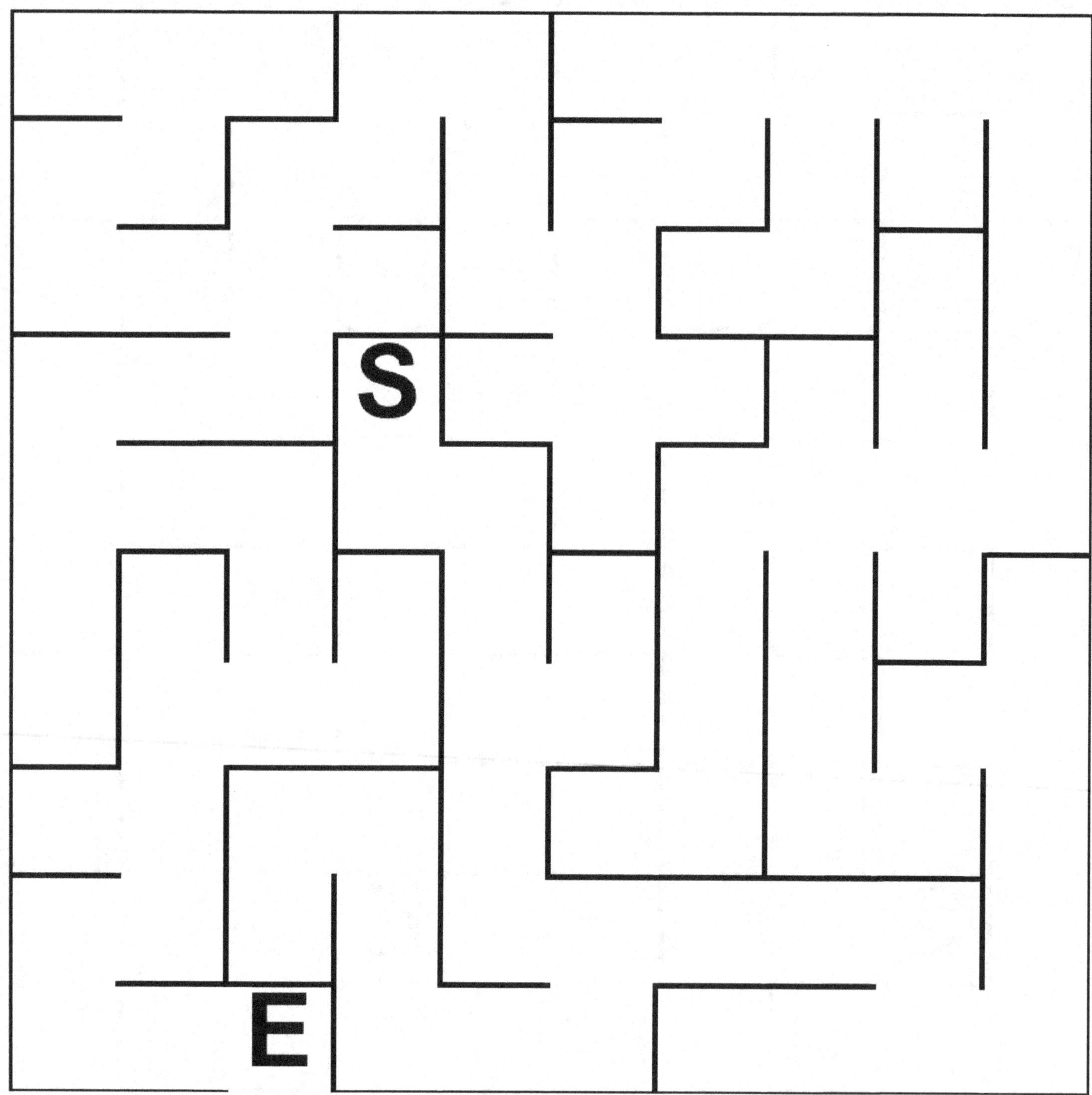

S
E

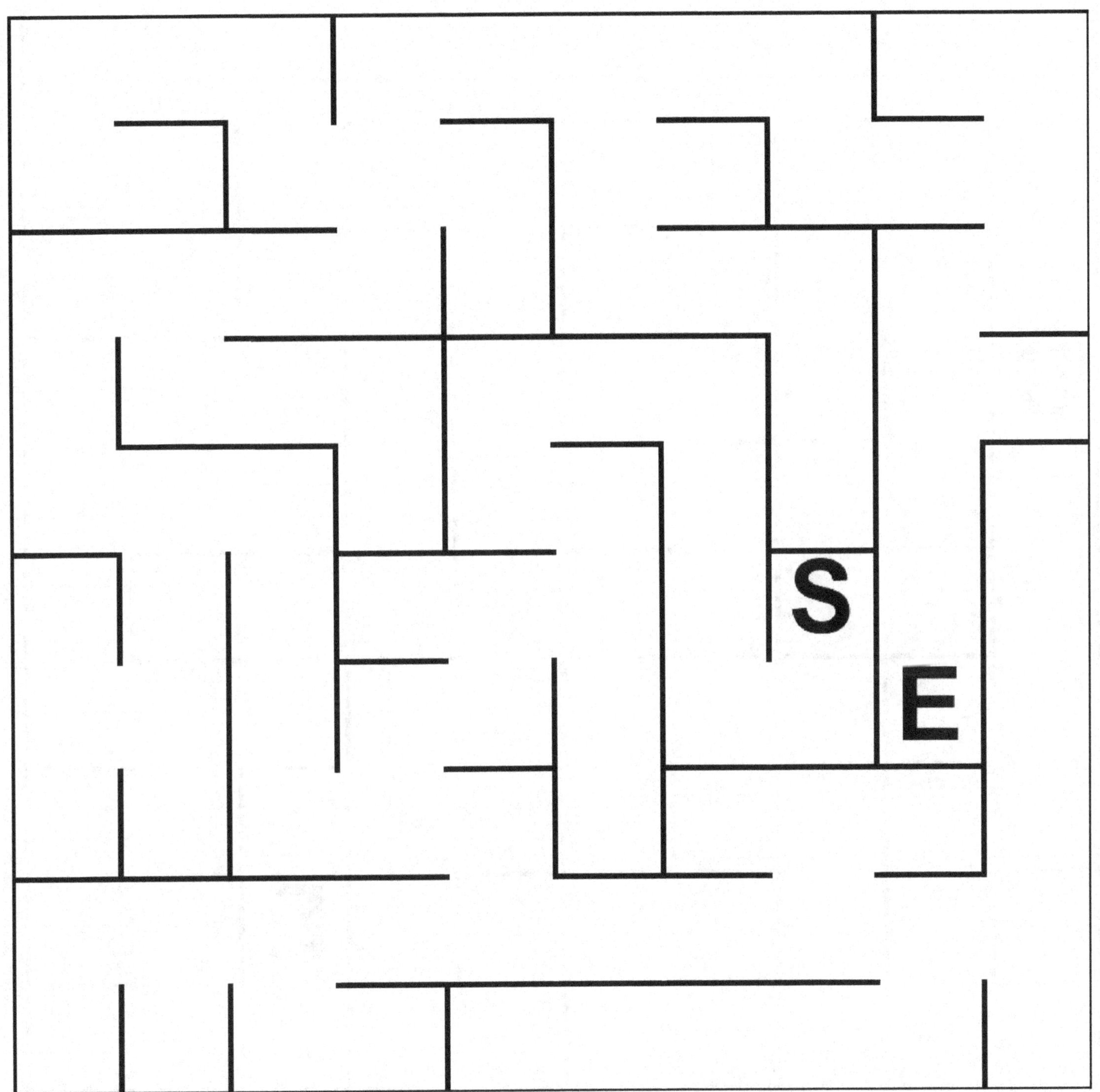

S
E

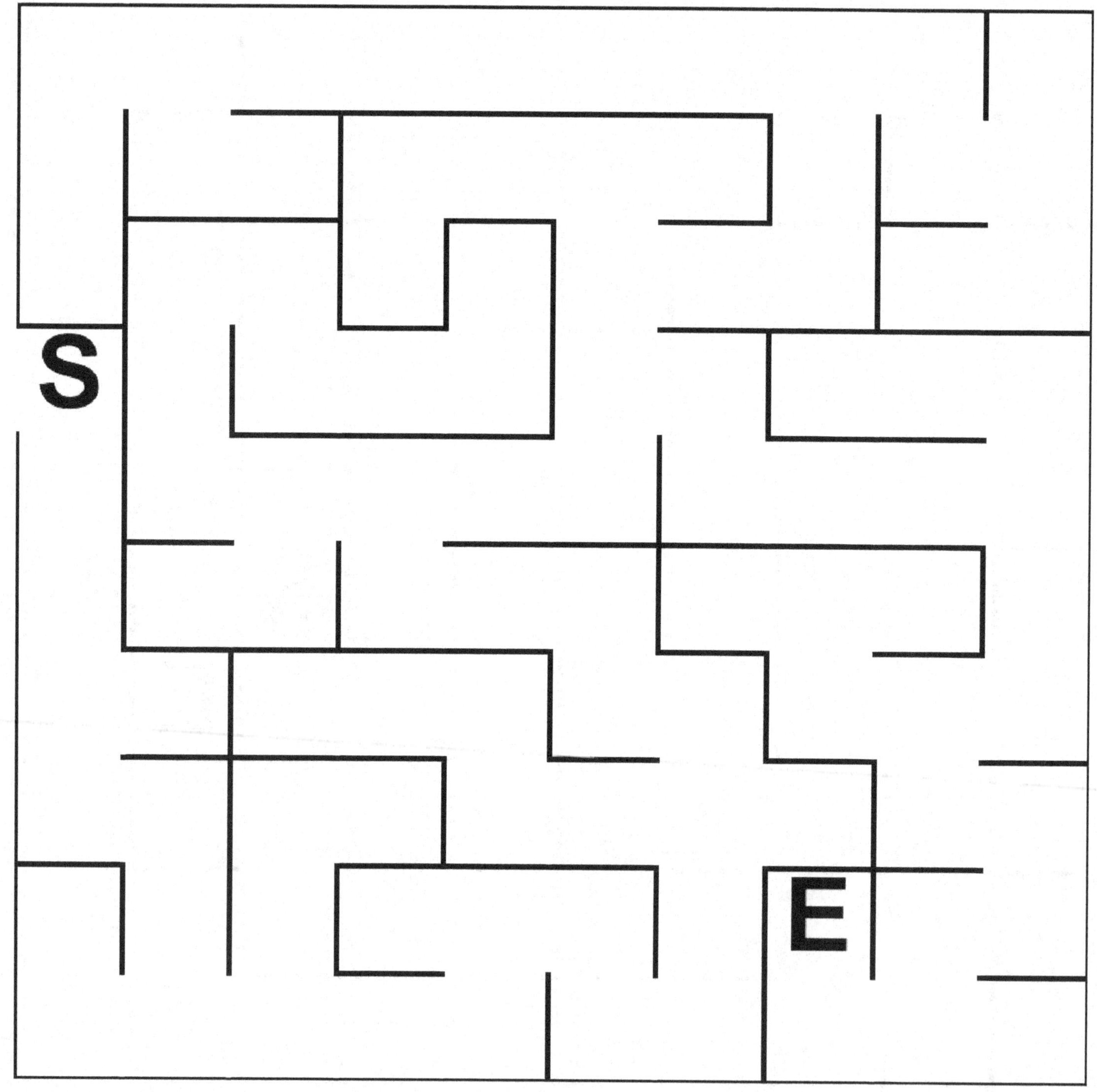

S
E

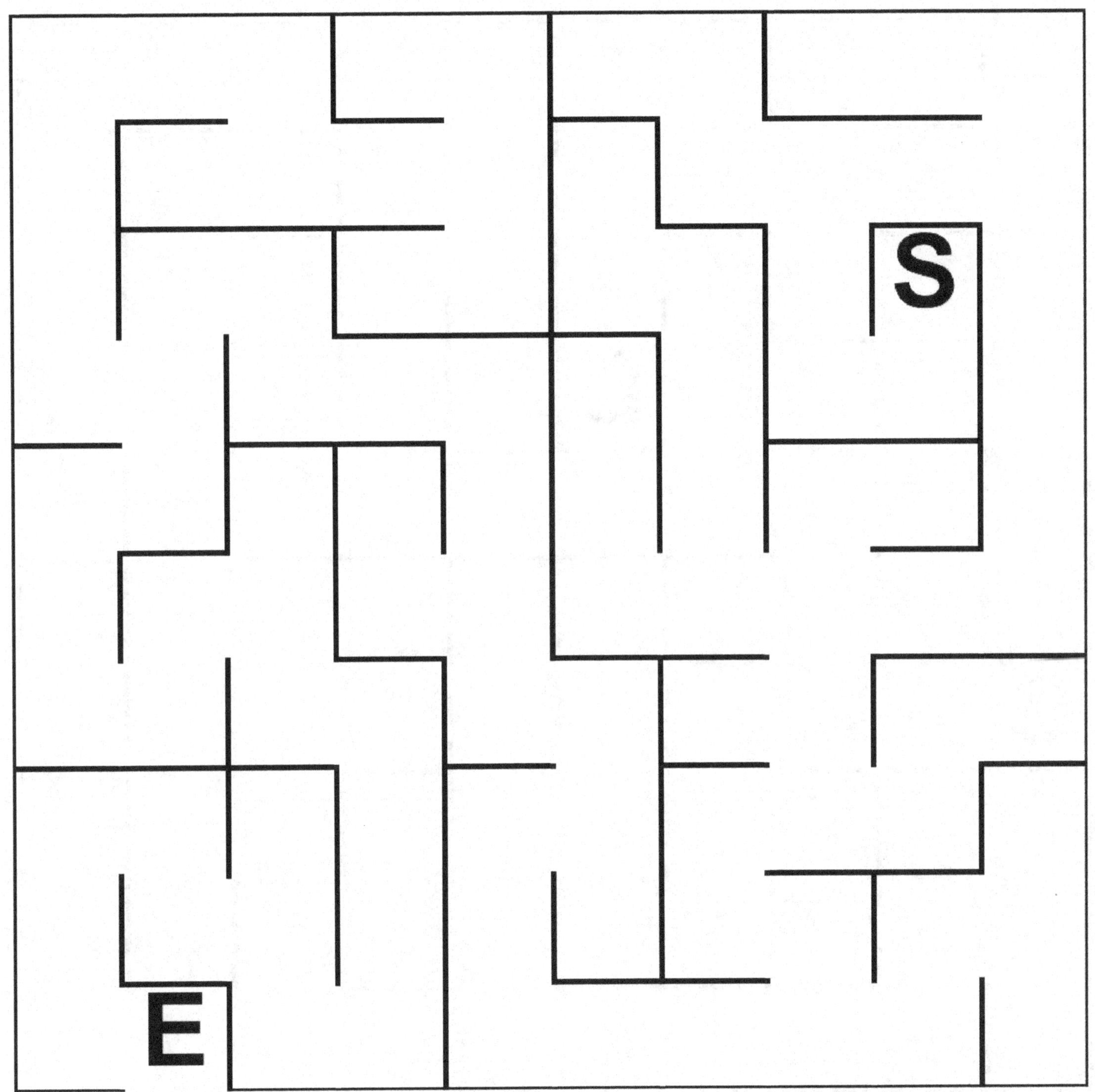

S
E

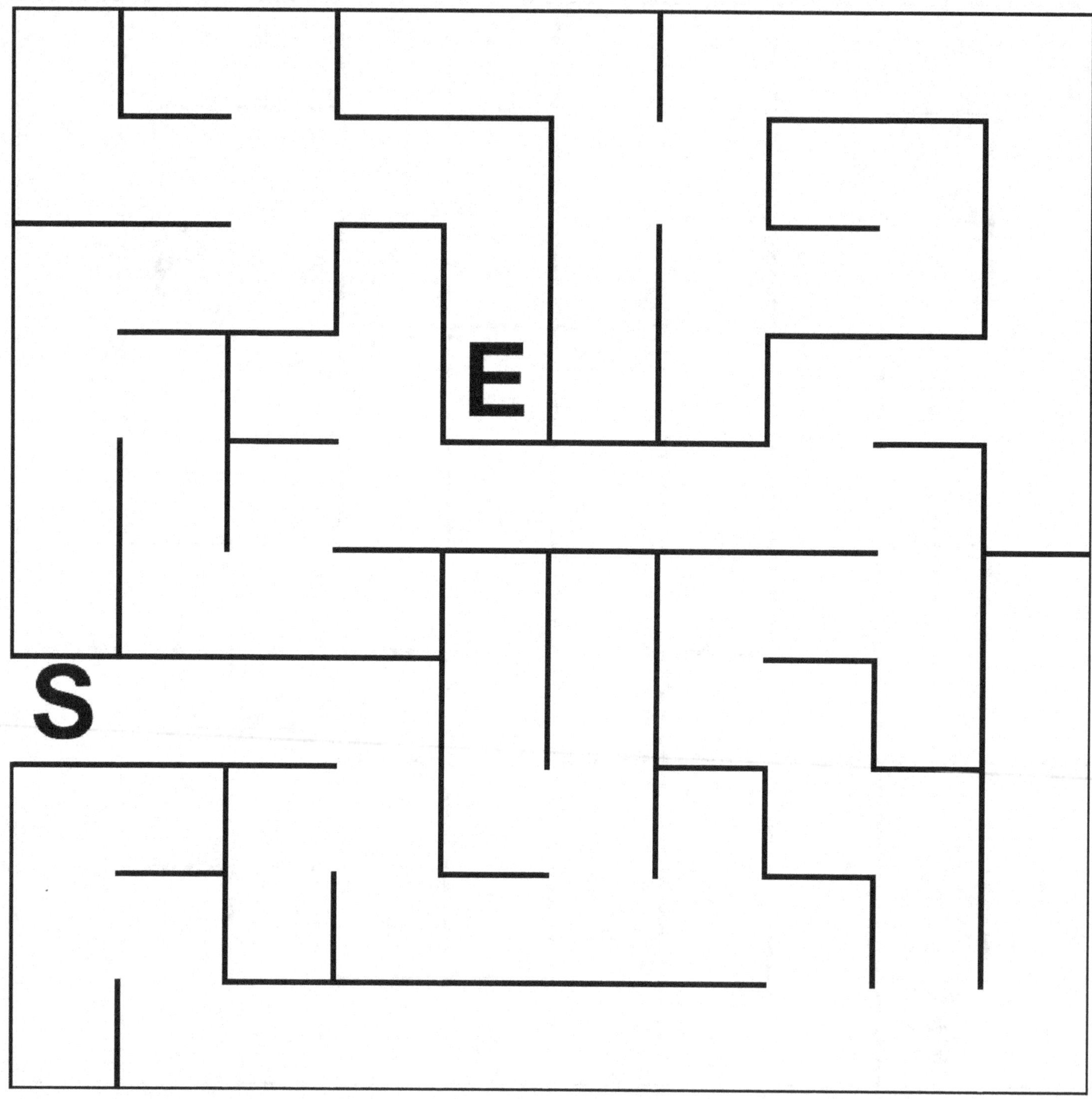

E
S

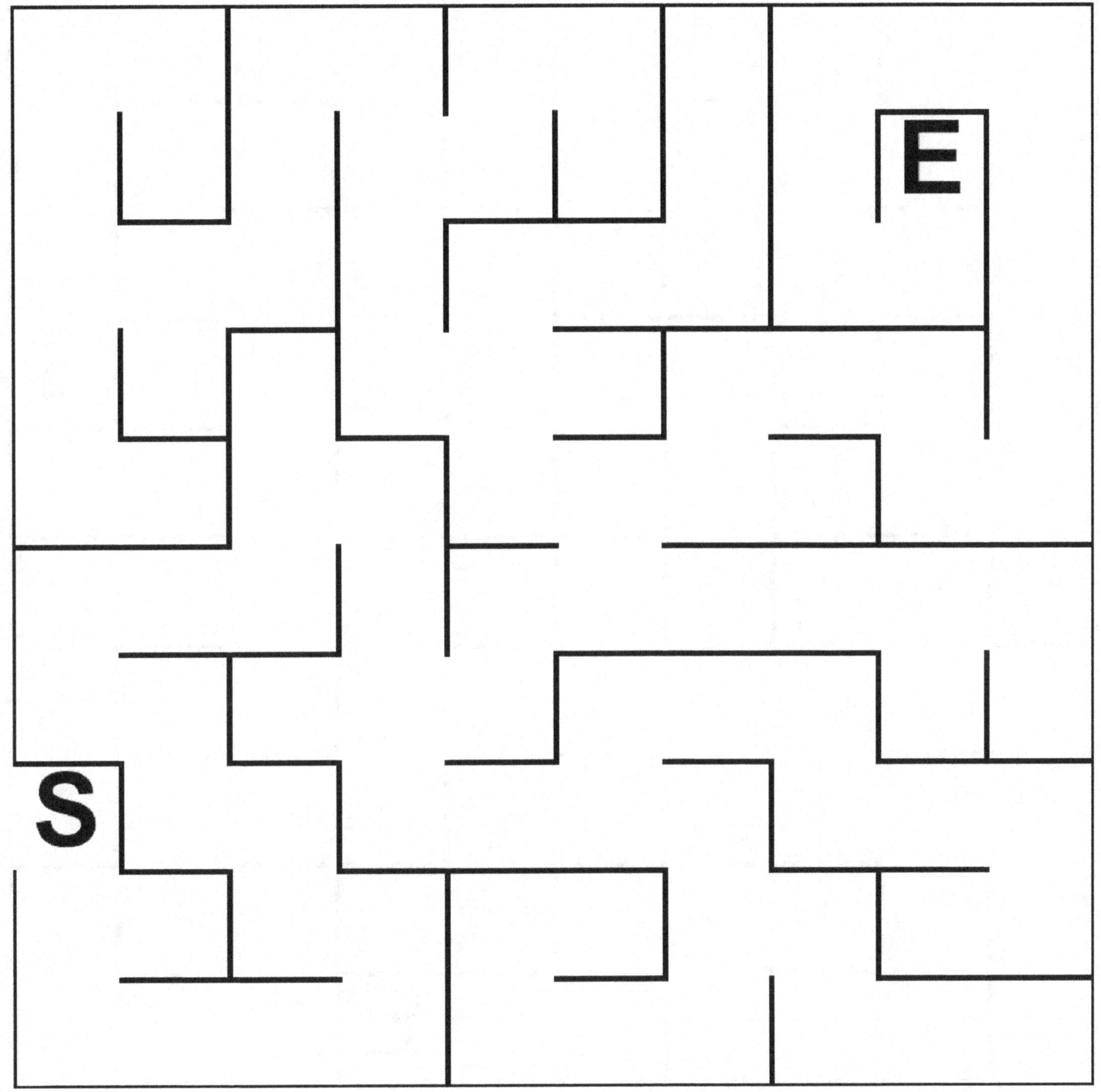

E
S

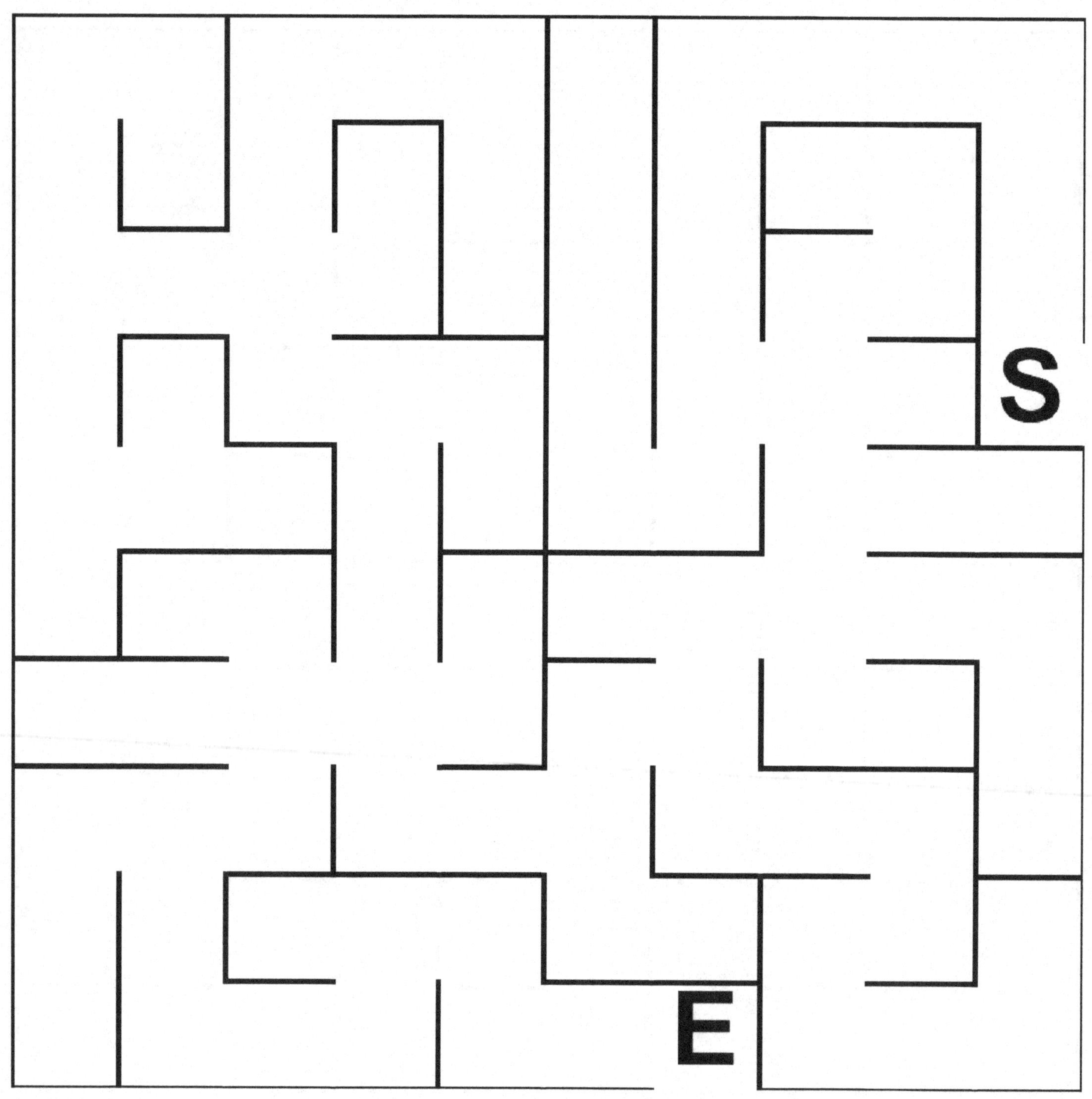
S
E

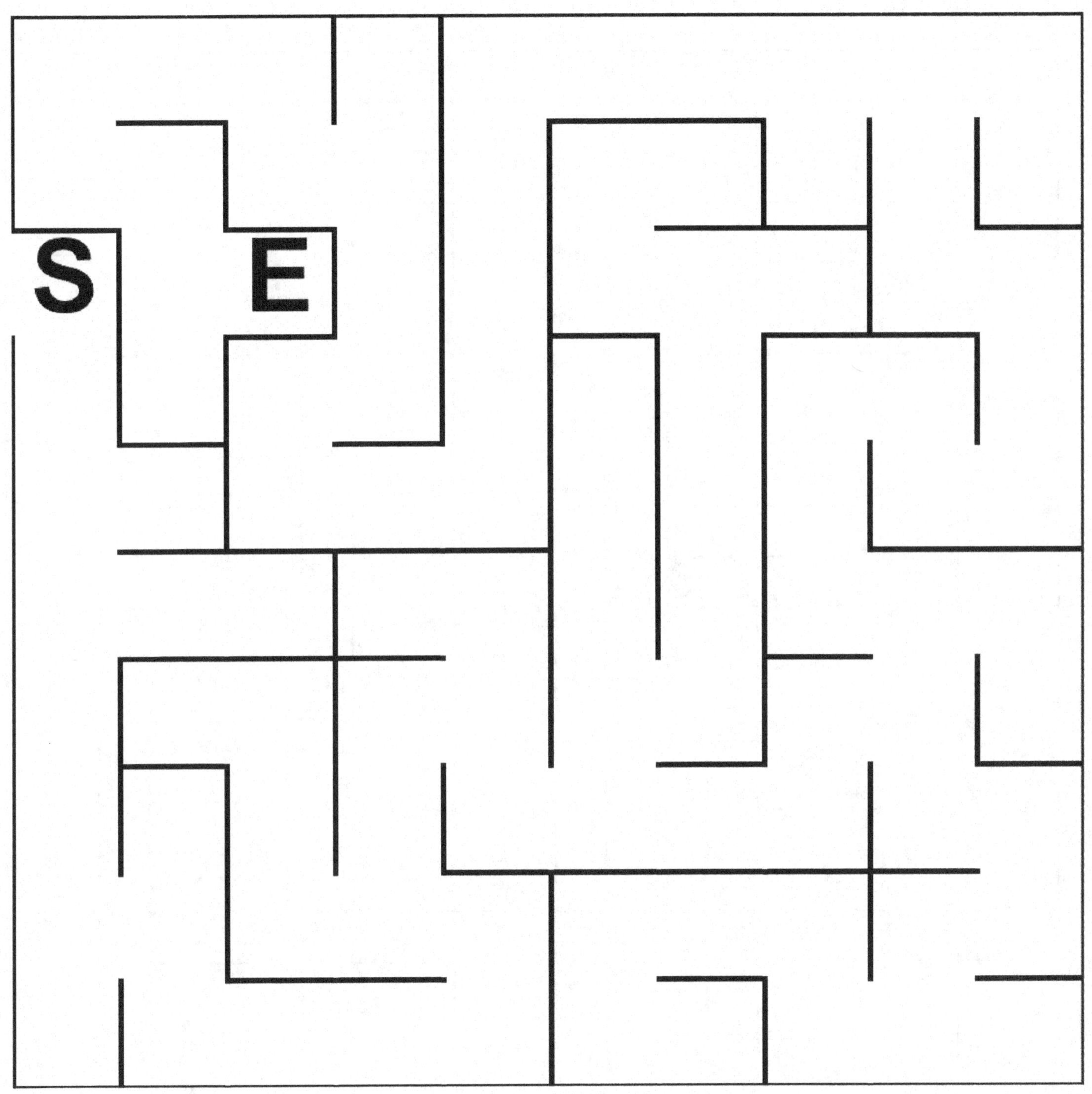

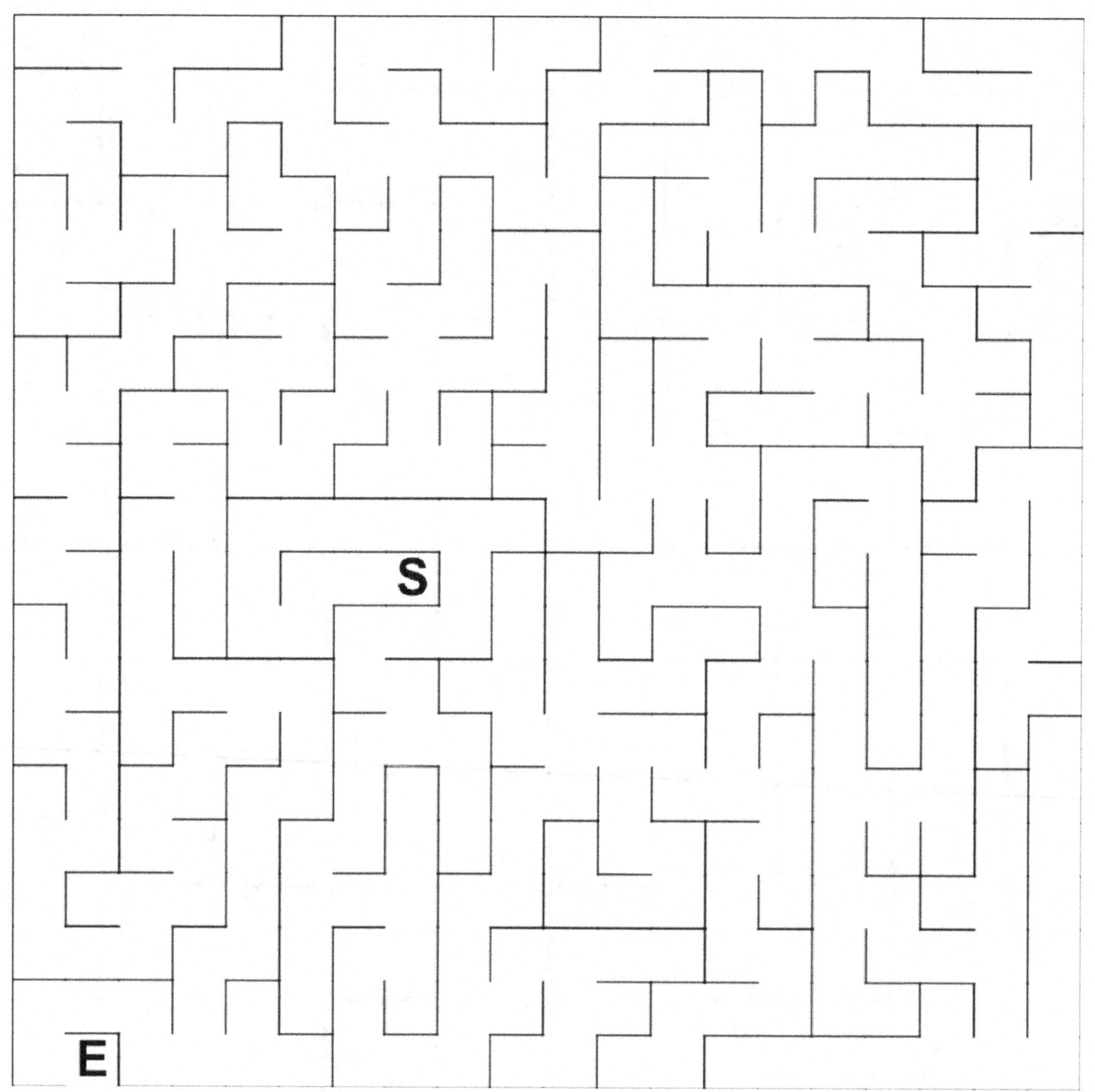

S
E

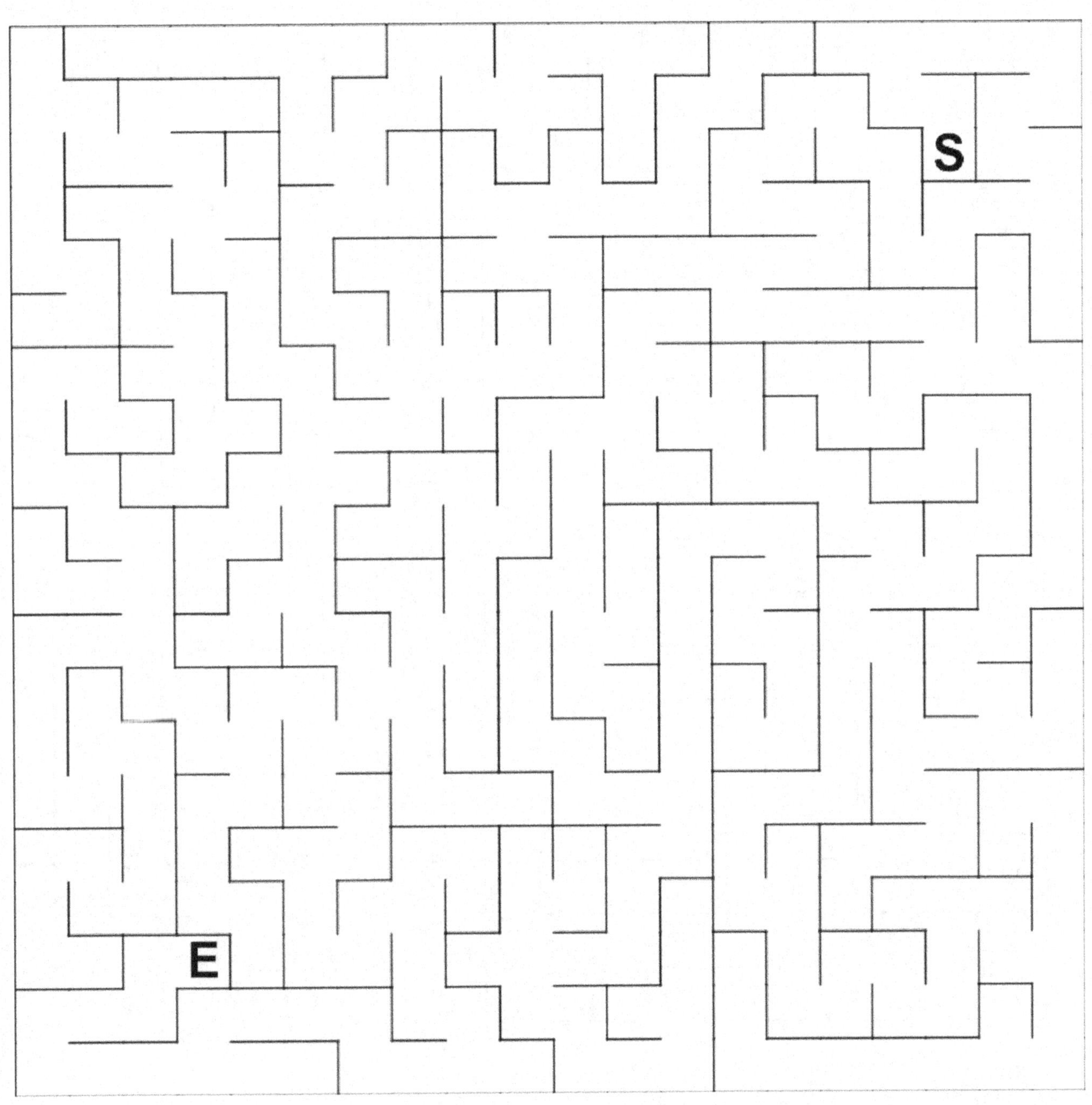

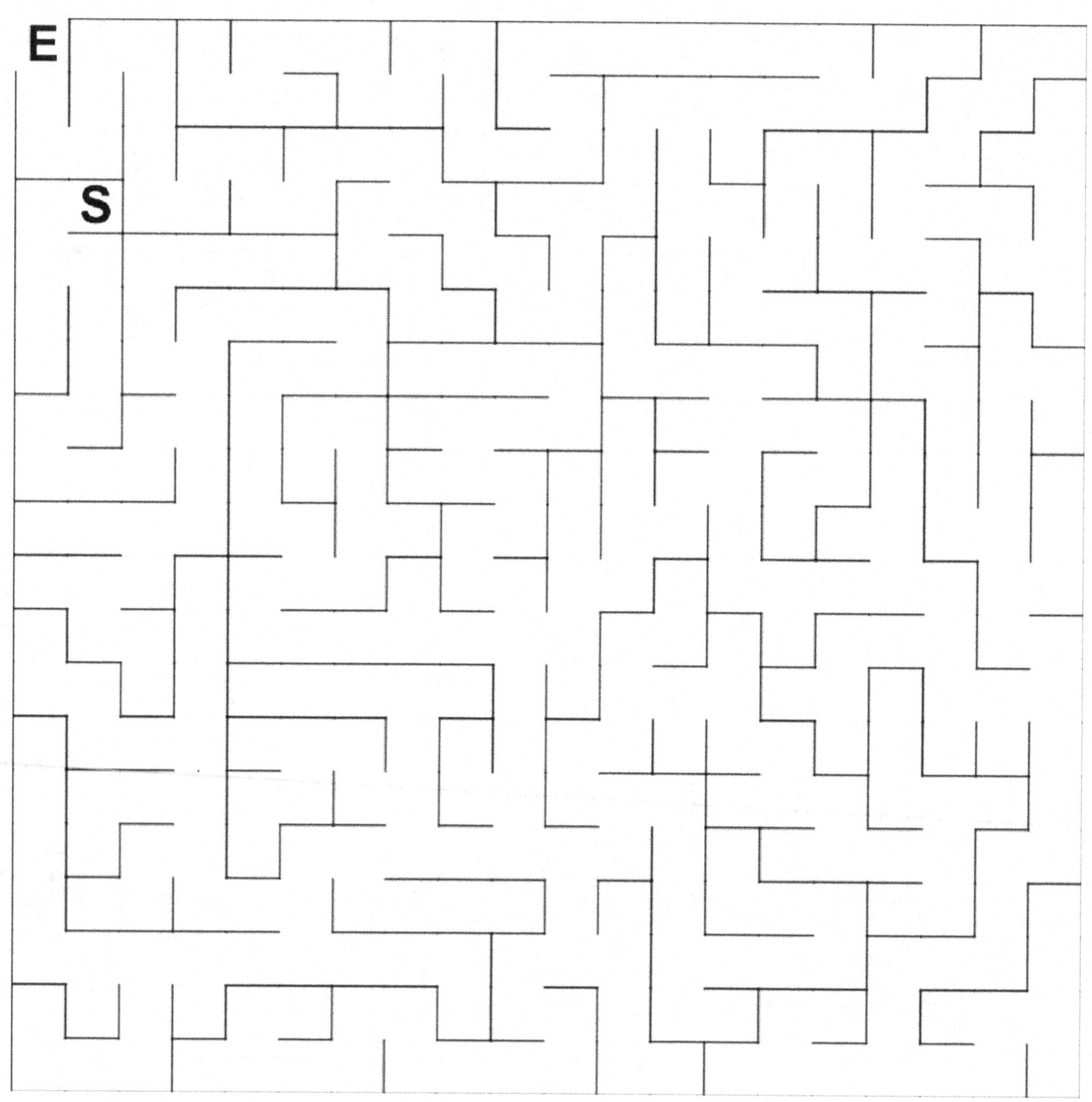
E
S

67

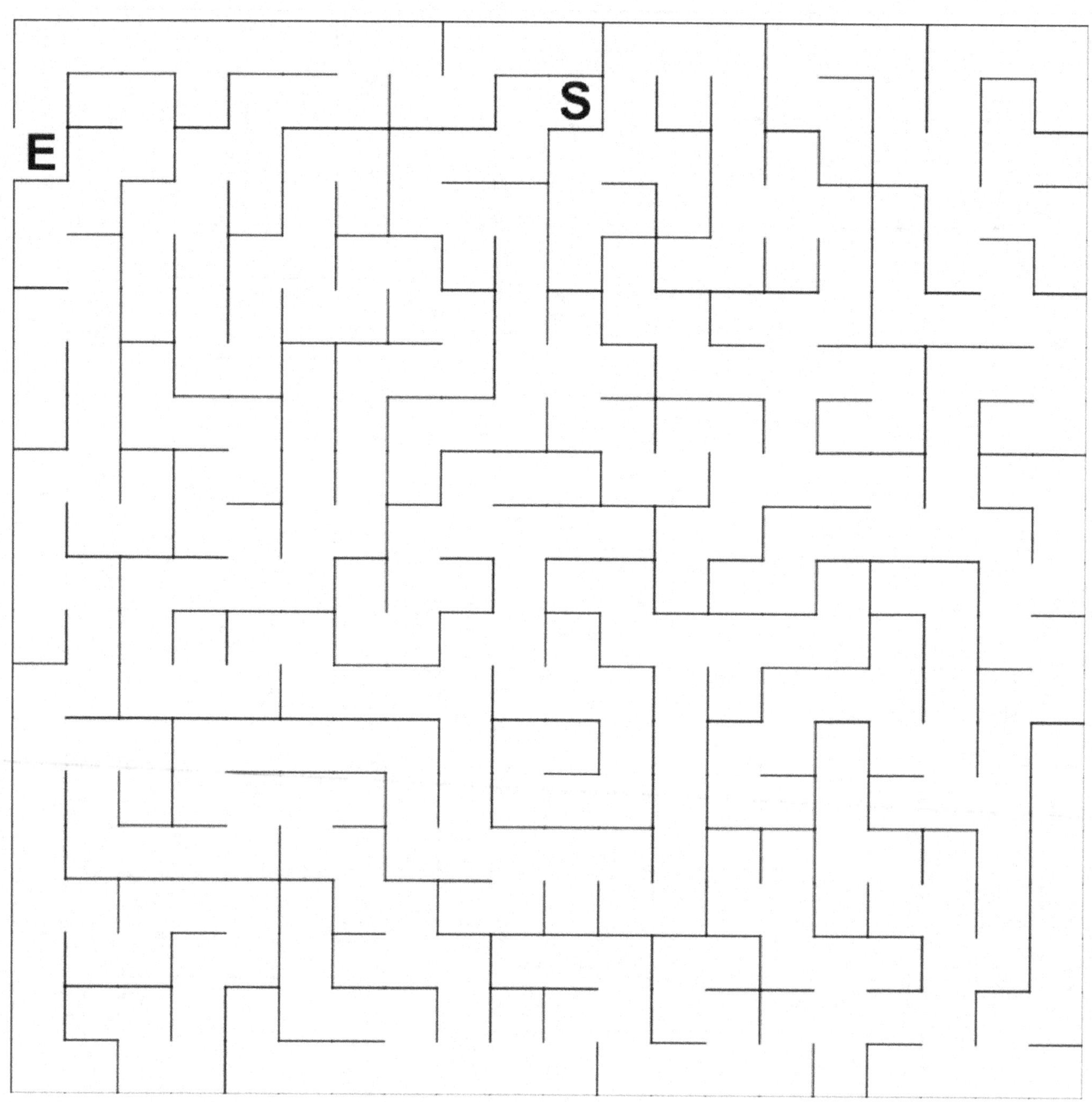

E
S

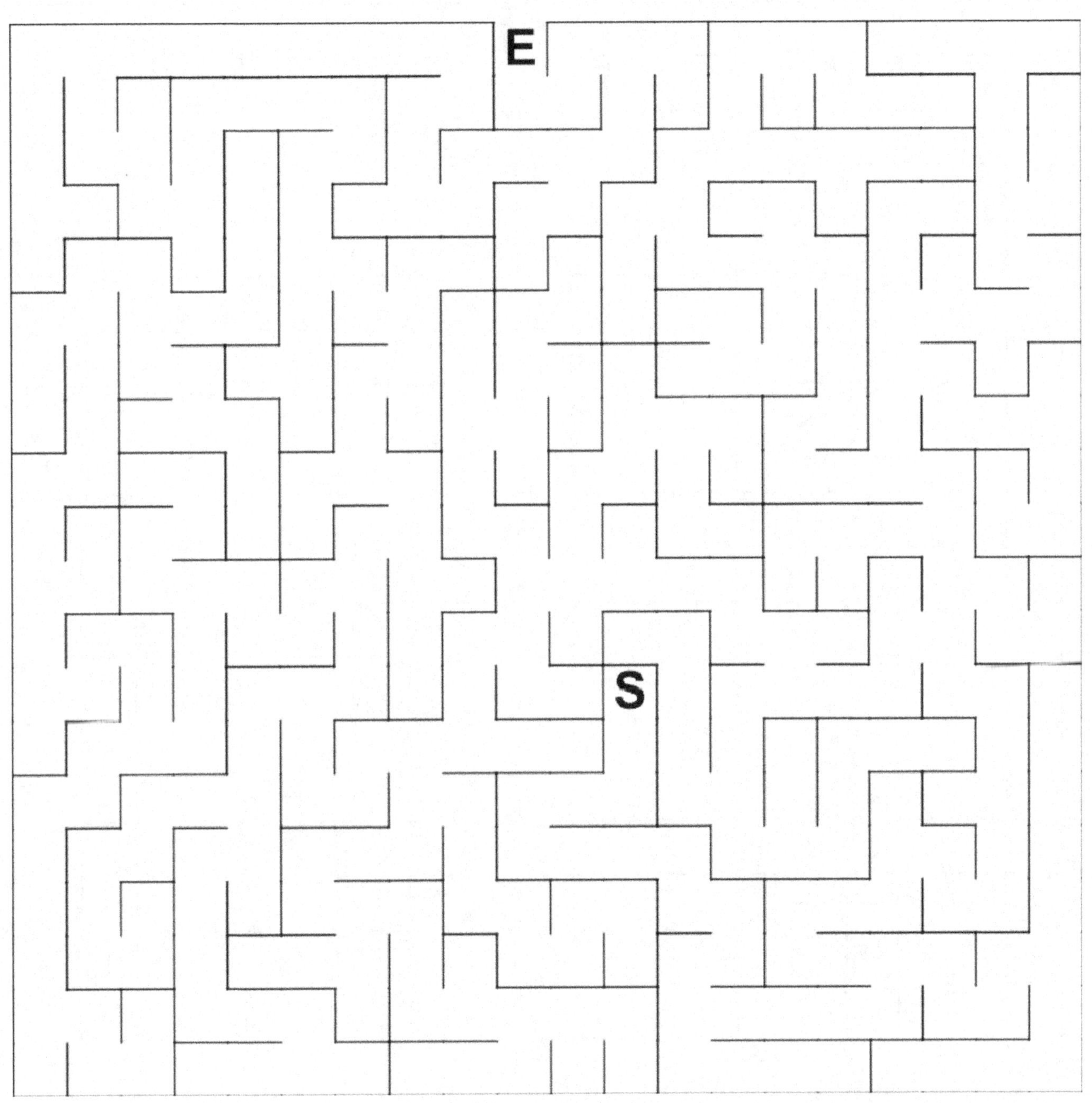

E
S

E
S

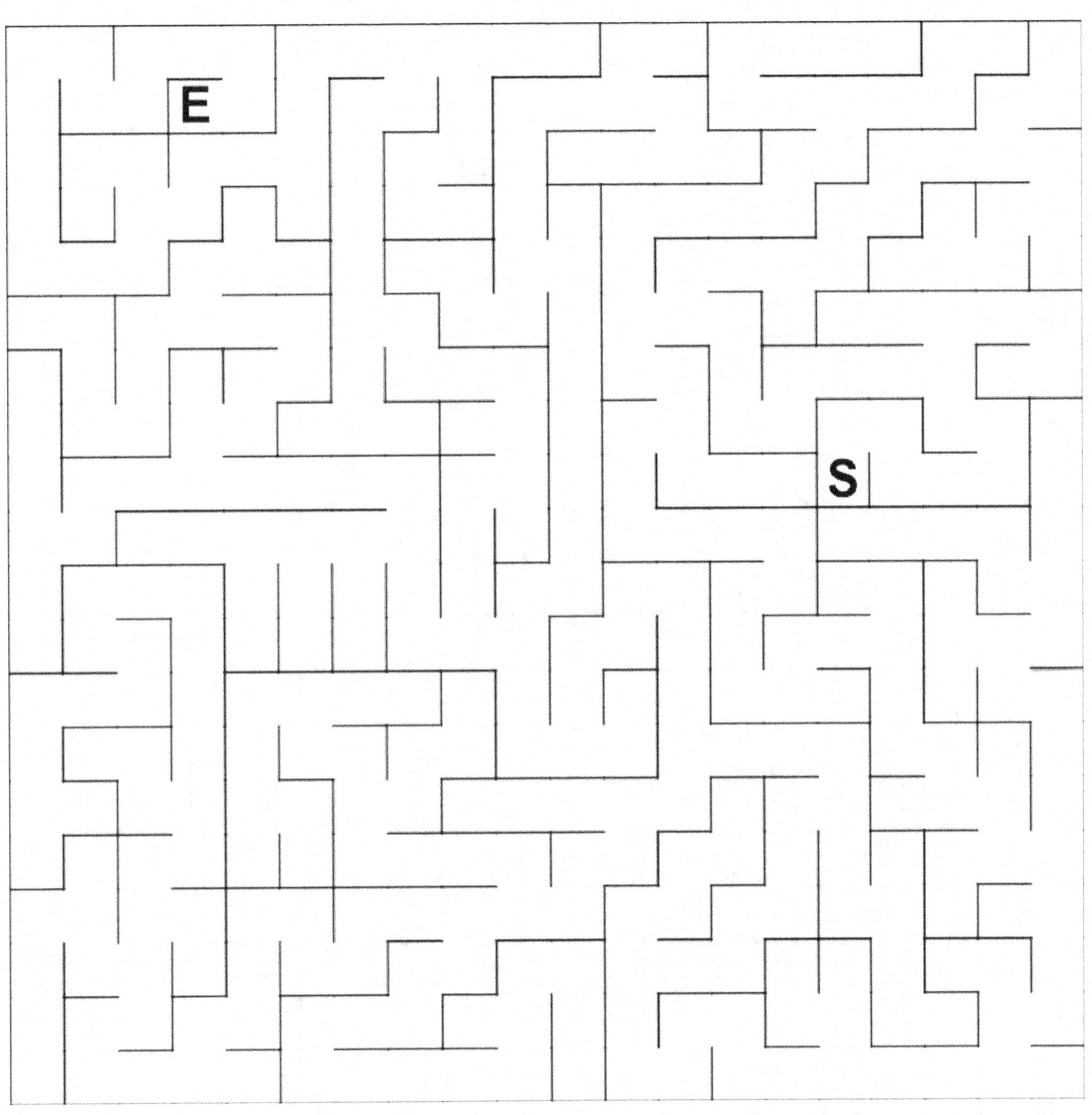

E
S

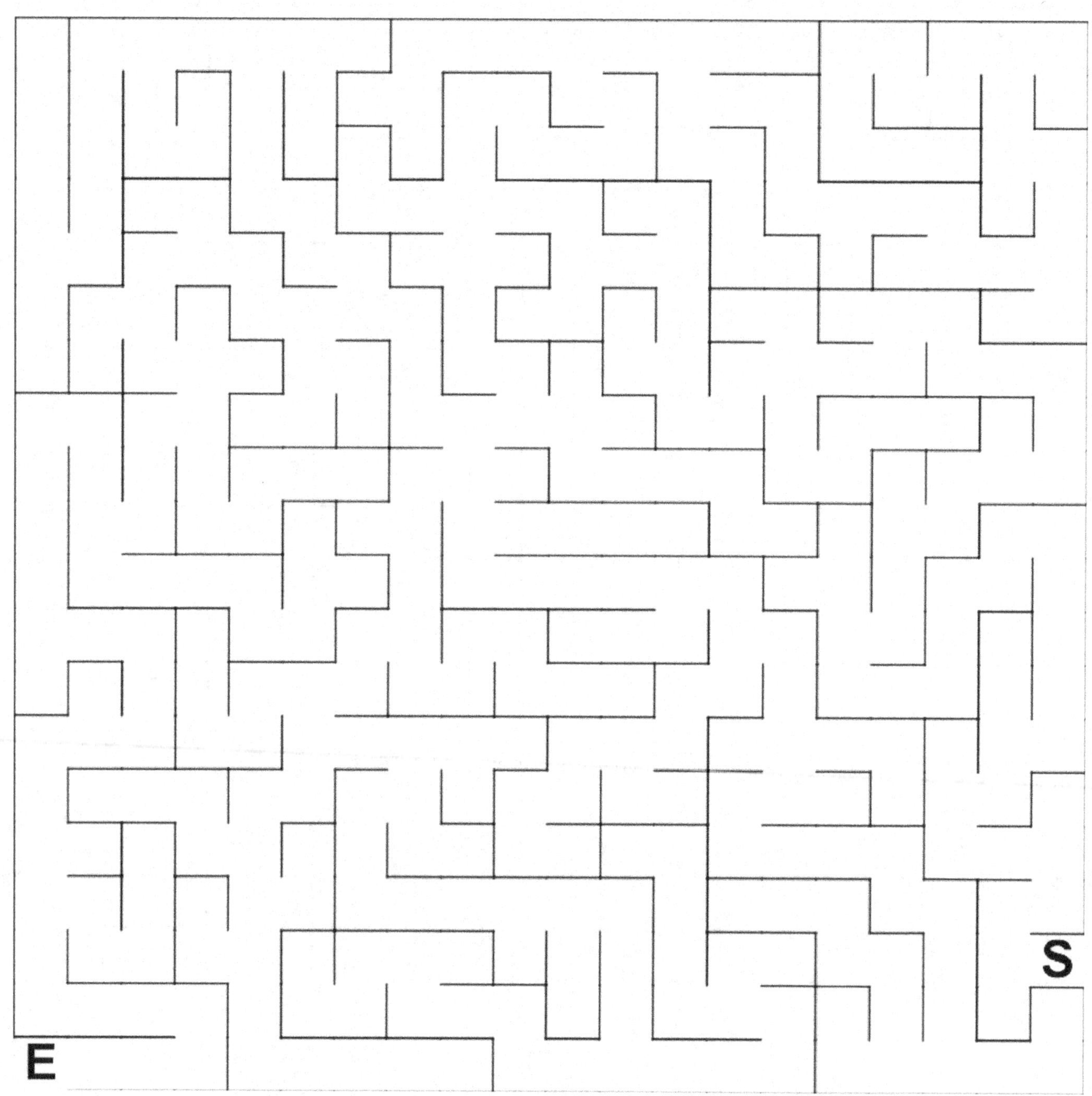

72

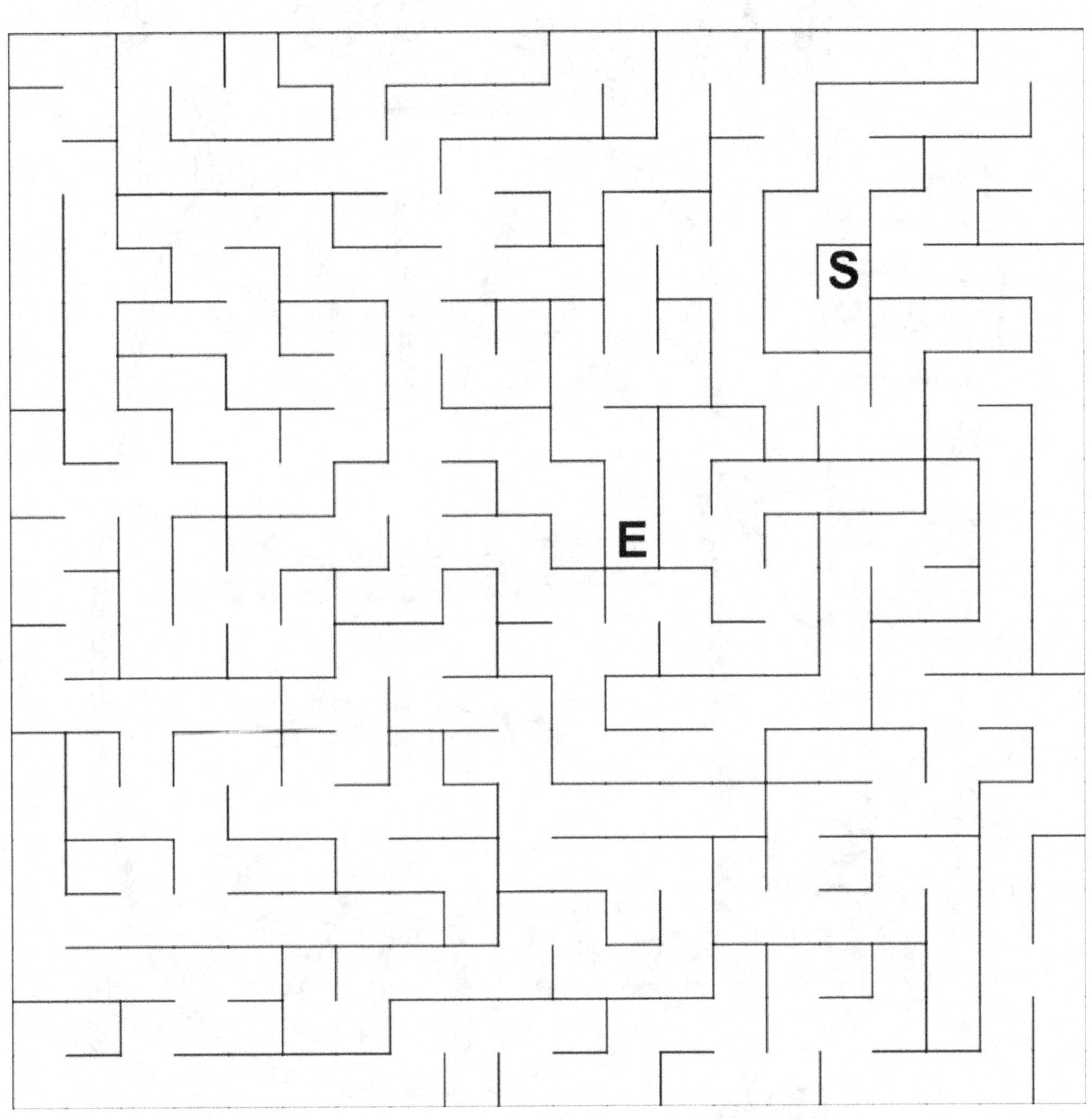
S
E

Search
words

Puzzle #1

COLORS WORD SEARCH

```
E  G  N  A  R  O  G  S  V  E
Z  E  L  A  P  B  R  H  T  P
N  A  R  B  C  R  E  A  M  A
L  E  M  O  N  O  Y  D  Y  S
P  D  E  R  I  W  T  E  Z  T
U  L  K  R  B  N  A  Y  C  E
R  E  E  J  G  H  D  T  M  L
P  R  C  U  O  W  H  I  T  E
L  R  D  B  L  A  C  K  G  K
E  D  K  E  D  B  F  I  F  O
```

BLACK	BLUE
BROWN	CREAM
CYAN	GOLD
GREEN	GREY
INDIGO	LEMON
ORANGE	PALE
PASTEL	PURPLE
RED	SHADE
WHITE	

ANIMAL WORD SEARCH

```
D  T  G  T  Y  N  N  U  B  C
I  R  I  O  P  P  I  H  M  S
T  A  O  G  D  N  L  D  O  Q
M  N  W  T  E  B  P  E  U  U
C  R  A  M  A  R  I  E  S  I
Z  A  X  H  O  G  A  R  E  R
E  B  T  X  P  N  I  M  D  R
B  B  K  F  O  E  K  L  I  E
R  I  H  S  I  F  L  E  A  L
A  T  N  O  I  L  H  E  Y  R
```

ALIGATOR	BIRD
BUNNY	CAT
DEER	DOG
ELEPHANT	FISH
FOX	GOAT
HIPPO	LION
MONKEY	MOUSE
RABBIT	SQUIRREL
TIGER	ZEBRA

WINTER WORD SEARCH

```
T  B  K  F  J  A  C  K  E  T
S  O  D  P  T  L  I  U  Q  N
C  O  R  E  B  M  E  C  E  D
A  T  L  B  L  Z  T  B  C  A
R  S  C  L  T  S  R  L  P  Q
F  N  W  A  I  A  T  B  E  A
W  O  O  N  P  H  H  A  C  M
I  W  O  K  J  N  C  F  O  G
N  C  L  E  N  I  A  R  L  C
D  R  E  T  A  E  H  Z  D  H
```

BLANKET	BOOTS
CAP	CHILL
COAT	COLD
DECEMBER	FOG
HAT	HEATER
ICE	JACKET
MELT	QUILT
RAIN	SCARF
SLED	SNOW
WIND	WOOL

SPORTS WORD SEARCH

```
L  Y  F  O  O  T  B  A  L  L
R  L  E  R  U  N  N  I  N  G
P  E  L  K  S  I  N  N  E  T
C  G  C  A  C  J  U  D  O  O
R  O  S  C  B  O  X  I  N  G
I  L  Z  P  O  E  H  N  U  O
C  F  H  Z  R  S  S  G  D  P
K  D  A  R  T  B  O  A  R  D
E  C  Y  C  L  I  N  G  B  H
T  G  G  N  I  M  M  I  W  S
```

BASEBALL	BOXING
CRICKET	CYCLING
DARTBOARD	FOOTBALL
GOLF	HOCKEY
JUDO	RUNNING
SOCCER	SWIMMING
TENNIS	

FOOTBALL WORD SEARCH

```
B  B  F  U  L  L  B  A  C  K
G  O  A  L  D  O  S  Q  G  H
R  Q  H  C  P  R  O  I  B  A
E  E  Q  A  K  U  A  W  D  N
F  C  S  M  L  F  J  U  I  D
E  P  U  N  T  F  I  A  G  O
R  V  B  C  E  N  T  E  R  F
E  L  B  M  U  F  W  I  L  F
E  L  D  R  I  V  E  O  M  D
H  U  D  D  L  E  Z  D  D  E
```

BACKFIELD	CENTER
DEFENSE	DOWN
DRIVE	FULLBACK
FUMBLE	GOAL
GUARD	HALF TIME
HANDOFF	HUDDLE
PUNT	REFEREE

BATMAN WORD SEARCH

V	S	P	E	N	G	U	I	I
Z	H	E	R	I	D	D	L	E	R
N	P	O	L	E	S	Y	H	M	N
P	I	N	A	M	O	W	T	A	C
C	V	B	E	L	T	K	A	I	Q
S	M	H	O	Z	F	L	G	F	C
J	O	K	E	R	E	R	E	G	X
P	R	R	P	N	S	E	E	B	W
S	V	J	E	V	A	C	R	D	A
R	Y	I	V	H	B	B	S	F	N

ALFRED	BANE
BELT	CATWOMAN
CAVE	CITY
FREEZE	HEROS
JOKER	PENGUIN
POLES	RIDDLER
ROBIN	

INSECT WORD SEARCH

```
P  H  O  R  S  E  F  L  Y  C
B  D  D  B  P  T  E  B  D  O
X  U  L  E  F  S  Y  B  R  C
F  V  T  E  M  T  A  V  A  K
I  Q  T  T  M  O  N  W  G  R
R  F  C  L  E  A  T  A  O  O
E  X  V  E  W  R  Y  H  N  A
F  G  I  A  E  L  F  F  F  C
L  C  I  C  A  D  A  L  L  H
Y  T  E  K  C  I  R  C  Y  Y
```

ANT	BEE
BEETLE	BUTTERFLY
CICADA	COCKROACH
CRICKET	DRAGONFLY
FIREFLY	FLEA
HORSEFLY	MAYFLY
MOTH	WASP

CAREER WORD SEARCH

I	A	N	R	E	I	H	S	A	C
C	A	R	P	E	N	T	E	R	L
A	N	D	B	R	D	I	Z	A	E
L	C	E	P	B	E	L	Q	W	R
T	A	N	I	A	F	V	I	R	K
X	S	T	L	N	Z	L	I	U	E
N	K	I	O	K	O	O	C	R	B
V	A	S	T	E	S	R	U	N	D
K	U	T	B	R	E	Y	W	A	L
M	R	E	M	R	A	F	R	B	H

ARTIST	BANKER
BUILDER	CARPENTER
CASHIER	CLERK
COOK	DENTIST
DRIVER	FARMER
LAWYER	NURSE
PILOT	

Puzzle #9

VEGETABLE WORD SEARCH

```
B  R  L  E  T  T  U  C  E  P
R  K  V  P  E  P  P  E  R  T
O  M  U  N  G  B  E  A  N  B
C  A  R  R  O  T  U  D  F  E
C  P  E  G  A  B  B  A  C  E
O  E  A  L  F  A  L  F  A  T
L  A  S  P  A  R  A  G  U  S
I  O  C  U  C  U  M  B  E  R
B  E  A  N  S  M  A  I  Z  E
O  C  O  R  N  S  R  W  M  L
```

ALFALFA	ASPARAGUS
BEANS	BEETS
BROCCOLI	CABBAGE
CARROT	CORN
CUCUMBER	LETTUCE
MAIZE	MUNGBEAN
PEA	PEPPER

SPRING WORD SEARCH

```
G  R  E  E  N  S  Y  H  B  Q
U  A  D  U  B  H  R  A  I  N
S  A  P  R  I  L  C  A  M  F
S  E  E  H  G  N  O  O  C  Y
Y  R  V  Z  C  N  B  O  F  I
S  N  E  A  E  R  I  Z  M  G
J  A  N  W  E  E  A  R  Q  R
F  C  U  U  O  L  R  M  P  A
F  N  H  S  B  L  U  B  X  S
B  U  T  T  E  R  F  L  Y  S
```

APRIL	BLOOM
BREEZE	BUD
BULBS	BUNNY
BUTTERFLY	FLOWERS
GRASS	GREEN
LEAVES	MARCH
MAY	RAIN
SPRING	

Puzzle #11

BIRD WORD SEARCH

```
H  E  N  I  U  G  N  E  P  L
X  E  L  I  T  O  R  R  A  P
P  G  N  G  R  O  W  L  I  N
I  I  N  B  A  S  Z  G  R  O
G  D  D  O  V  E  M  Y  L  S
E  D  G  U  C  L  N  Z  B  T
O  I  A  N  C  L  K  A  C  R
N  K  W  A  H  K  A  O  R  I
R  H  N  I  B  O  R  F  O  C
H  H  D  L  K  W  U  G  W  H
```

CRANE	CROW
DOVE	DUCK
EAGLE	FALCON
GOOSE	HAWK
KIWI	OSTRICH
OWL	PARROT
PENGUIN	PIGEON
ROBIN	

UNICORN WORD SEARCH

B	I	M	A	G	I	C	Y	G	B
E	K	R	E	W	O	L	F	A	S
A	V	S	D	D	P	I	N	K	E
U	Y	E	D	H	R	W	A	N	D
T	R	P	I	U	E	E	V	O	L
I	Z	A	P	L	O	A	A	A	I
F	B	Y	T	A	E	L	R	M	X
U	Q	J	S	S	H	B	C	T	S
L	U	F	R	O	L	O	C	N	K
N	F	W	R	E	T	T	I	L	G

BEAUTIFUL	BELIEVE
CLOUDS	COLORFUL
DREAMS	FLOWER
GLITTER	HAPPY
HEART	LOVE
MAGIC	PINK
STAR	WAND

SEA ANIMAL WORD SEARCH

```
W  M  M  F  I  S  H  B  Y  S
I  J  E  L  L  Y  F  I  S  H
K  H  O  C  T  O  P  U  S  A
F  R  E  T  S  Y  O  C  E  R
R  E  T  S  B  O  L  R  A  K
L  A  E  S  C  O  R  A  L  M
G  A  S  M  A  L  C  B  I  U
C  Z  R  N  I  H  P  L  O  D
E  C  O  R  M  O  R  A  N  T
R  B  T  Q  O  T  T  E  R  A
```

CLAMS	CORAL
CORMORANT	CRAB
DOLPHIN	FISH
JELLYFISH	LOBSTER
OCTOPUS	OTTER
OYSTER	SEAL
SEALION	SHARK

FAMILY WORD SEARCH

R	H	U	S	B	A	N	D	Y	D
B	E	Z	A	P	D	N	A	R	G
R	C	H	I	L	D	R	E	N	N
R	E	H	T	O	M	Q	X	H	E
E	E	H	C	O	U	S	I	N	P
S	C	F	T	O	R	N	N	N	H
D	L	I	I	A	L	B	C	Z	E
M	P	E	E	W	F	U	B	L	W
W	P	E	Y	N	T	N	U	A	E
A	M	D	N	A	R	G	J	F	U

AUNT	BROTHER
CHILDREN	COUSIN
FATHER	GRANDMA
GRANDPA	HUSBAND
MOTHER	NEICE
NEPHEW	UNCLE
WIFE	

BACK TO SCHOOL

```
P  H  V  E  Z  S  S  D  L  K
A  W  O  V  R  F  K  W  T  Y
P  S  Q  M  D  O  A  R  M  K
E  J  C  S  E  E  S  W  A  B
R  X  L  H  E  W  S  Q  T  M
R  O  A  I  O  D  O  S  H  A
N  B  S  M  C  O  A  R  A  O
L  E  S  S  O  N  L  R  K  P
J  V  Z  I  U  Q  E  E  G  O
T  P  R  I  N  C  I  P  A  L
```

CLASS	EXAM
GRADE	HOMEWORK
LESSON	MARKS
MATH	PAPER
PASSED	PENCIL
PRINCIPAL	QUIZ
SCHOOL	

FATHER\'S DAY WORD SEARCH

```
E   F   N   H   E   V   A   R   B   D
H   R   X   J   O   J   G   O   J   W
U   F   C   A   Y   L   O   O   V   Z
J   F   A   D   P   D   I   K   L   Q
L   R   R   M   Y   D   D   D   E   F
H   M   I   L   I   H   N   A   A   S
O   U   N   V   O   L   O   A   D   Y
M   V   G   N   F   V   Y   N   R   Q
E   D   L   S   I   J   E   F   O   G
Y   P   A   Z   F   A   T   H   E   R
```

BRAVE	CARING
DADDY	FAMILY
FATHER	GOLF
GRANDPA	HOLIDAY
HOME	HONOR
HUGS	JOKES
LOVE	

Puzzle #17

FRUIT WORD SEARCH

```
Z  Y  U  A  C  A  A  F  S  N
R  A  W  Q  O  S  P  O  R  V
M  I  T  O  C  I  R  P  A  D
E  Z  X  A  O  J  K  B  L  B
L  E  M  O  N  P  R  I  N  E
O  B  O  I  U  A  L  O  V  L
N  A  N  U  T  G  N  U  O  I
O  K  P  E  O  G  N  A  M  Q
I  Y  R  R  E  H  C  W  B  W
B  W  H  O  E  G  N  A  R  O
```

APPLE	APRICOT
BANANA	CHERRY
COCONUT	KIVI
LEMON	MANGO
MELON	ORANGE
PLUM	

PET WORD SEARCH

```
D E F U B L W P A O
G O A T R A R A H R
C A G E E M A R P O
K Q L W E B B R U D
I U N I D U B O Z E
T A C L T N I T S N
T R K D L N T W D T
E I U G S Y P P U P
N U N E K C I H C O
D M G O H E G D E H
```

AQUARIUM	BREED
BUNNY	CAGE
CAT	CHICKEN
DOG	FED
GOAT	HEDGEHOG
KITTEN	LAMB
PARROT	PAW
PUPPY	RABBIT
RODENT	WILD

Puzzle #19

BIRTHDAY WORD SEARCH

```
S  S  Y  C  W  H  S  B  S  J
F  N  D  A  G  I  H  Y  C  G
P  I  S  N  O  O  L  L  A  B
R  N  D  D  E  J  O  B  K  O
E  V  S  L  R  I  S  G  E  G
S  I  M  E  H  A  R  Q  P  A
E  T  V  S  H  A  C  F  A  M
N  E  F  E  K  S  P  J  R  E
T  P  U  I  G  O  I  P  T  S
W  S  C  T  G  F  U  W  Y  S
```

BALLOONS	CAKE
CANDLES	CARDS
FRIENDS	GAMES
GIFTS	HAPPY
INVITE	PARTY
PRESENT	WISHES

Puzzle #20

WEATHER WORD SEARCH

```
L   H   U   M   I   D   I   T   Y   N
O   I   Y   L   M   R   O   T   S   W
F   O   G   T   I   K   A   I   J   E
D   O   R   H   S   A   M   I   S   T
S   C   R   E   T   O   H   X   N   L
W   D   O   E   T   N   R   N   X   W
I   Z   U   F   C   L   I   F   U   V
N   S   N   O   W   A   E   N   Q   S
D   S   E   G   L   C   S   H   G   A
R   E   L   O   O   C   N   T   S   L
```

CLOUDS	COOLER
FOG	FORECAST
FROST	HAIL
HUMIDITY	LIGHTNING
MIST	RAIN
SHELTER	SNOW
STORM	SUN
WET	WIND

Coloring

Math
exercise

Addition For Kids

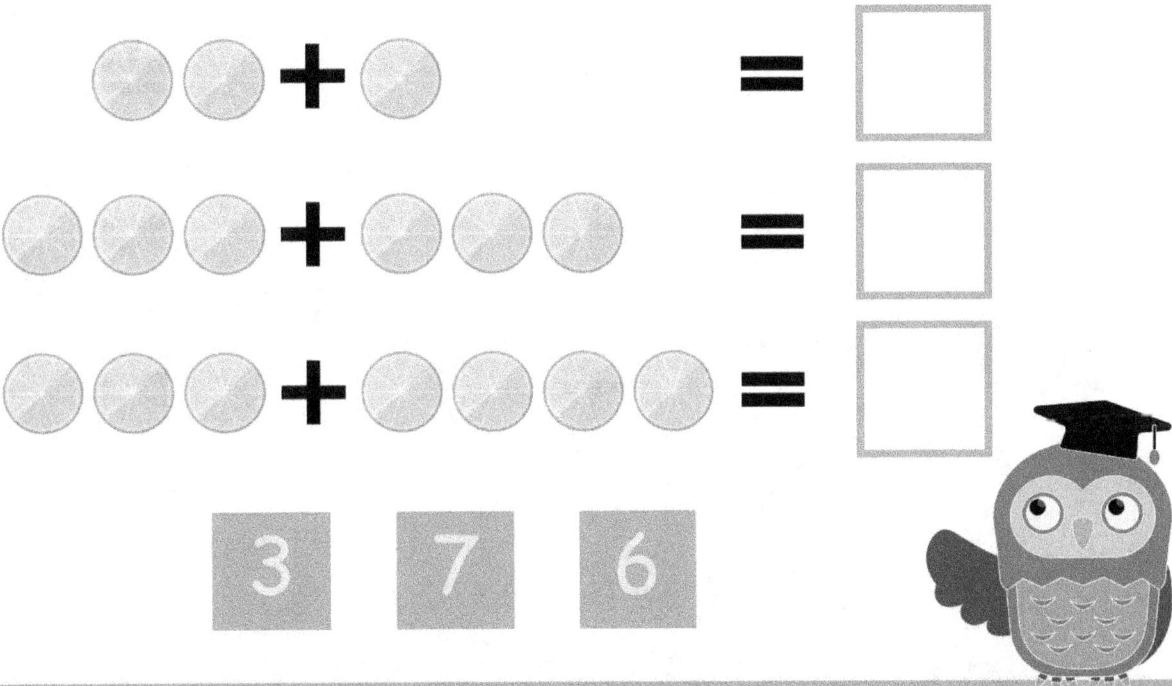

Addition For Kids

$$5 + 2 = \boxed{}$$

$$2 + 1 = \boxed{}$$

$$4 + 3 = \boxed{}$$

3   7   6

Addition For Kids

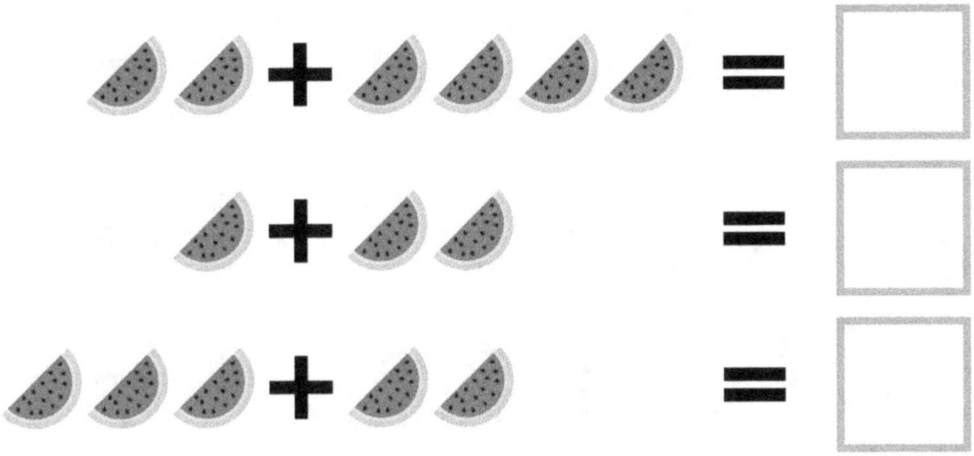

3 5 6

Addition For Kids

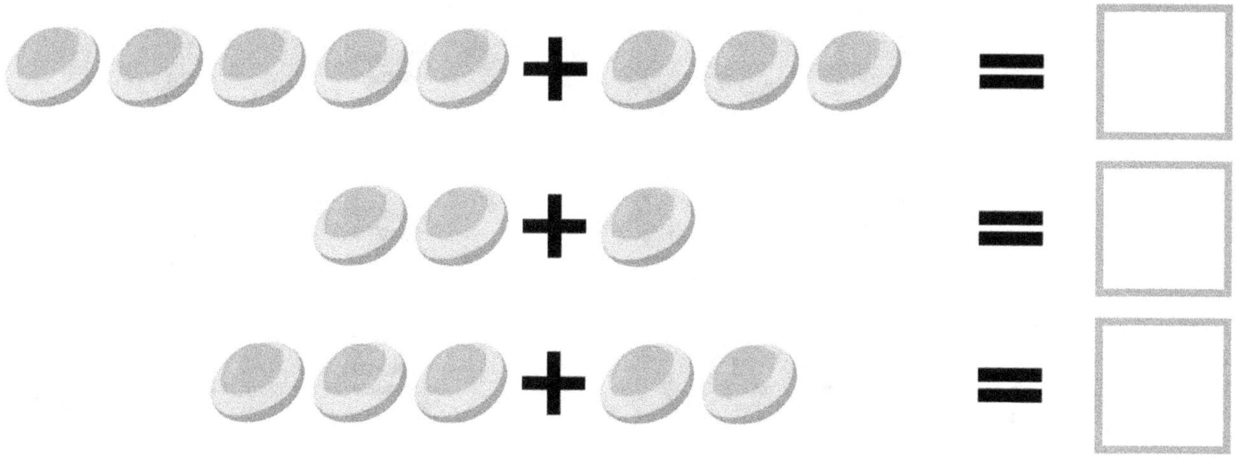

3 5 8

Addition For Kids

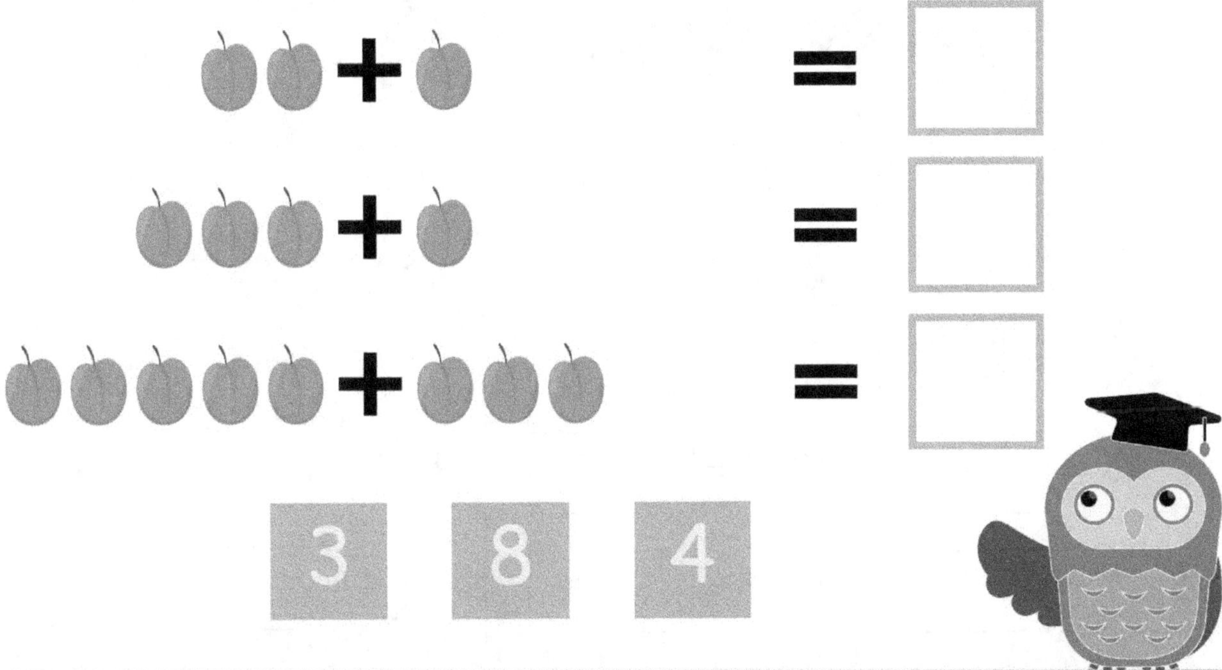

Fill in the missing numbers.

a.

b.

7 + 5 = [|]   12 - 7 = [|]

5 + 7 = [|]   12 - 5 = [|]

4 + 8 = [|]   12 - 4 = [|]

8 + 4 = [|]   12 - 8 = [|]

Fill in the missing numbers.

$12 = 3 + 7 + \boxed{}$ $\qquad$ $3 = 12 - 8 - \boxed{}$ $\qquad$ $12 = 20 - \boxed{} - 2$

$9 + 4 = \boxed{}$ $\qquad$ $12 - 4 = \boxed{}$ $\qquad$ $6 + 7 = \boxed{}$

$\boxed{} + 6 = 20$ $\qquad$ $12 - \boxed{} = 6$ $\qquad$ $7 + 7 = \boxed{}$

$\boxed{} = 12 + 6 - 8$ $\qquad$ $4 = 20 - 12 - \boxed{}$ $\qquad$ $\boxed{} = 7 + 2 + 1$

Complete the pictures to make 8.

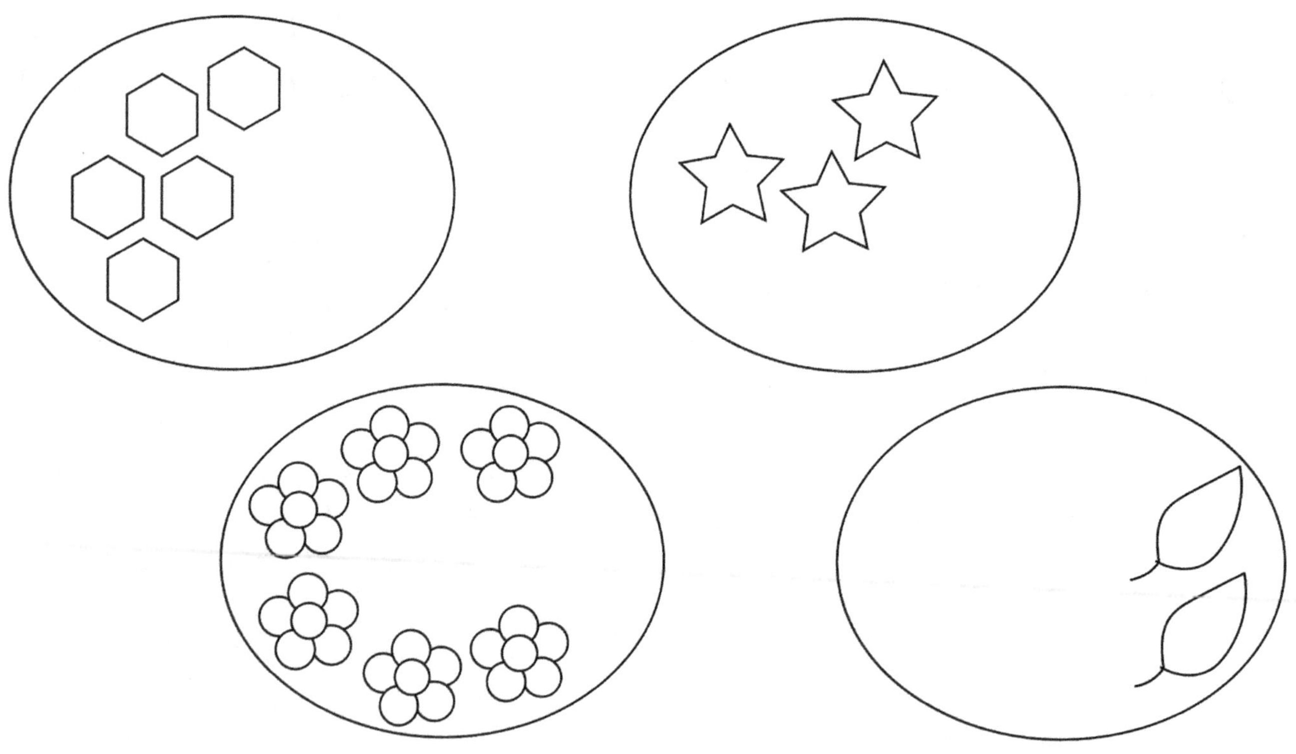

Match the Number

Draw a line from the number to the matching set of objects.

2

4

3

5

8

Counting

Count the objects. Write the correct number in the box. Color the objects for fun.

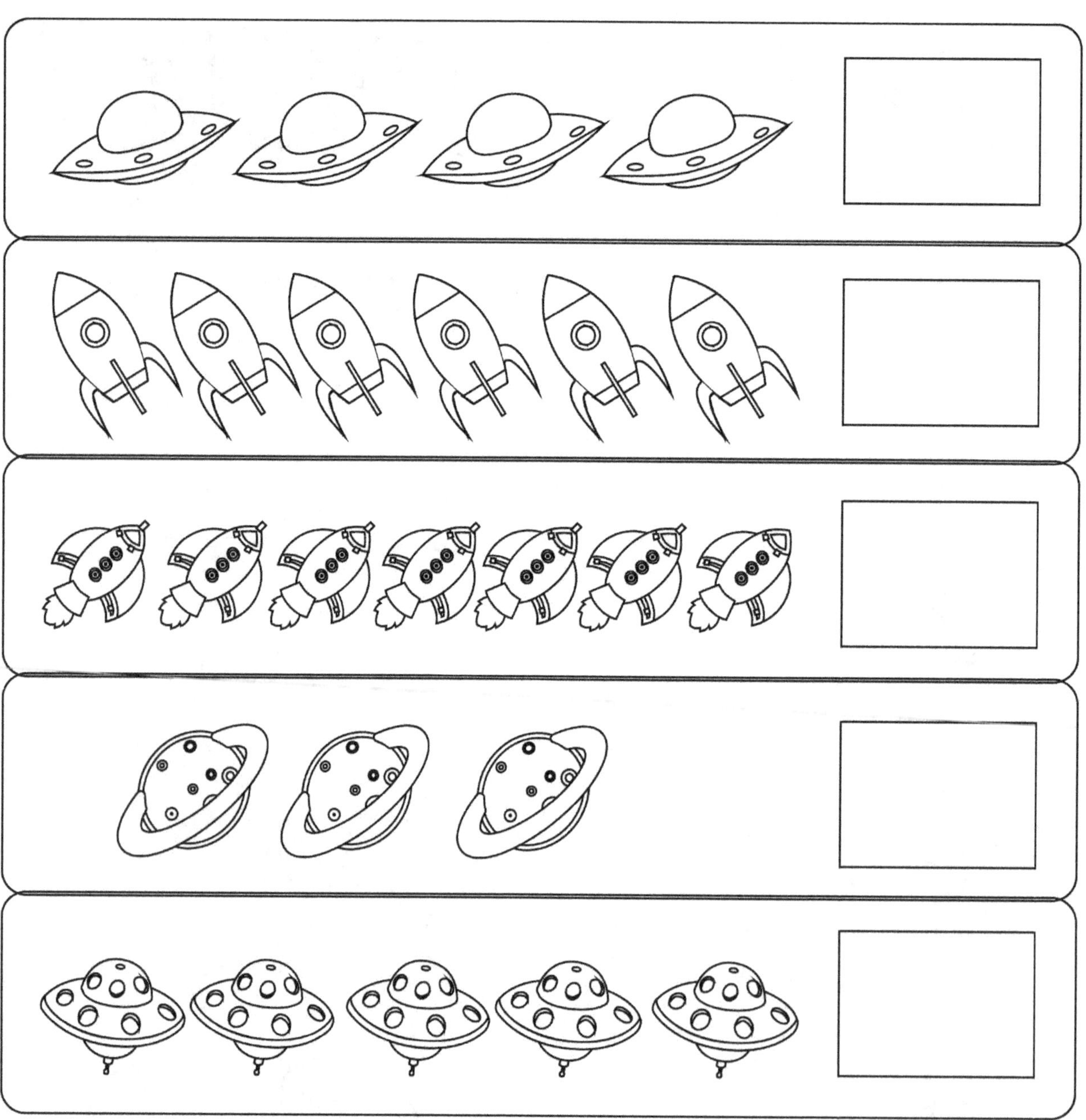

Coloring Addition

Find the answer tio each problem and write in the given box. Use the numbers to color the pictures.

$6 + 3 =$		Yellow	$5 + 2 =$		Blue
$4 + 4 =$		Green	$8 + 2 =$		Orange
$2 + 2 =$		Red	$3 + 2 =$		Pink

Subtract Numbers

Find the spaceship. Subtract the numbers in each box and color the spaceship with the correct answer.

6 - 3 = 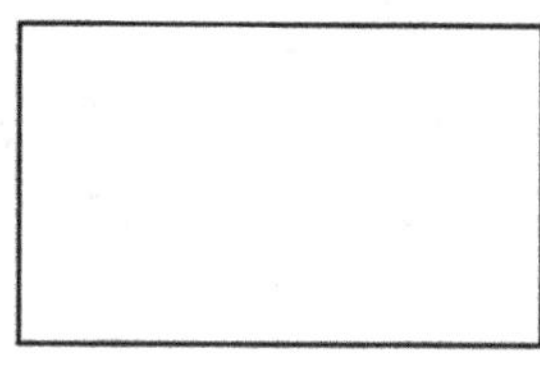 

8 - 5 = 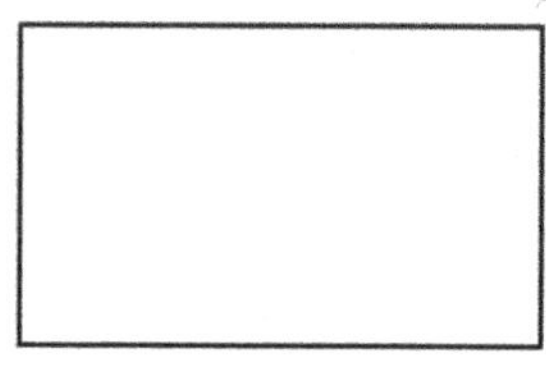 

4 - 2 = 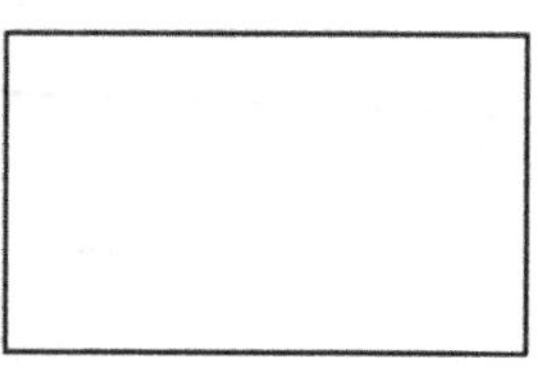 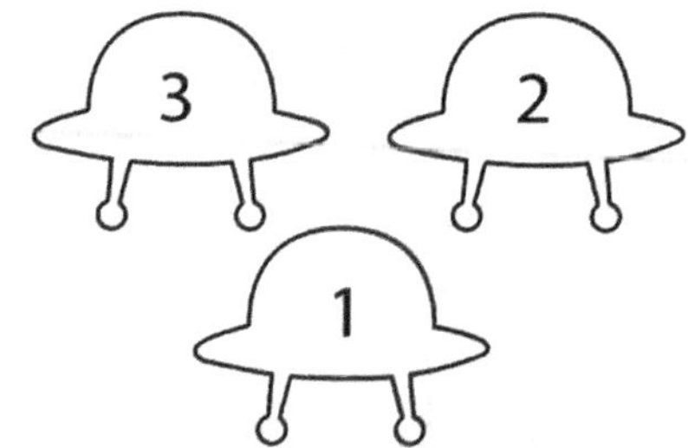

9 - 2 = 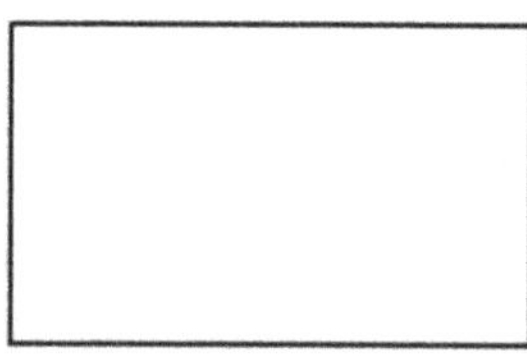 

Missing Numbers

Can you fill in the missing numbers by launching rocket to the space?

ARRANGE THE NUMBERS FROM THE SMALLEST TO THE LARGEST

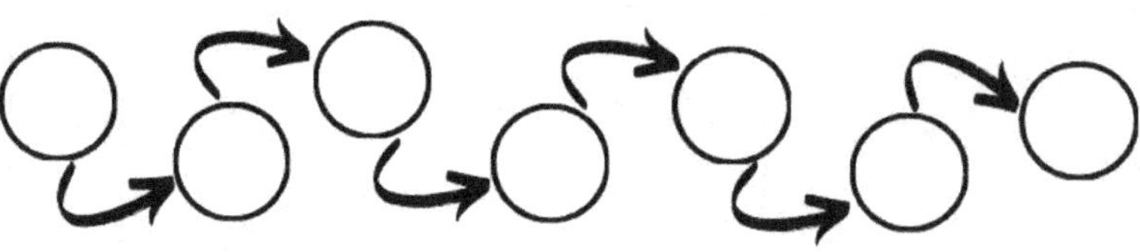

7-3-5-9-7-1-2

4-6-12-2-8-0-10

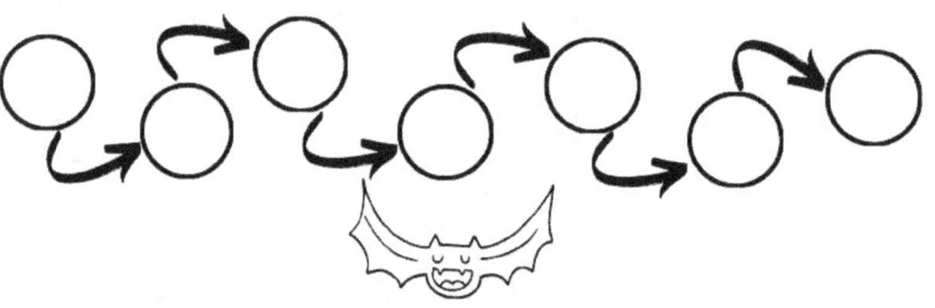

9-6-15-3-12-0-18

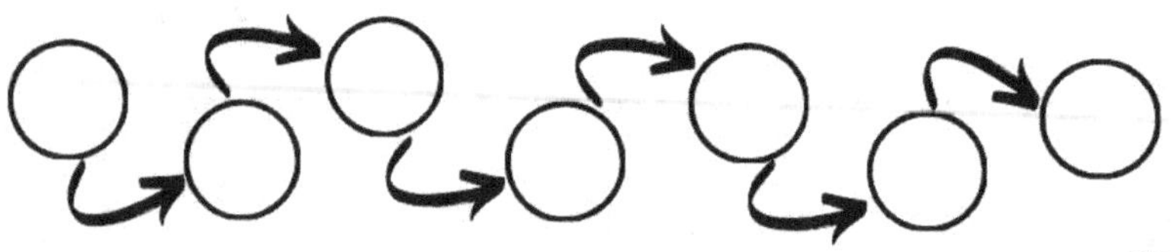

ADDITIONS

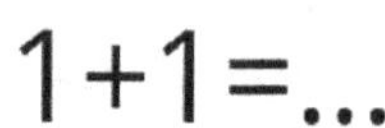

1+1=...	1+3=...
1+2=...	1+4=...
1+2=...	1+5=...

ARRANGE THE NUMBERS FROM THE SMALLEST TO THE LARGEST

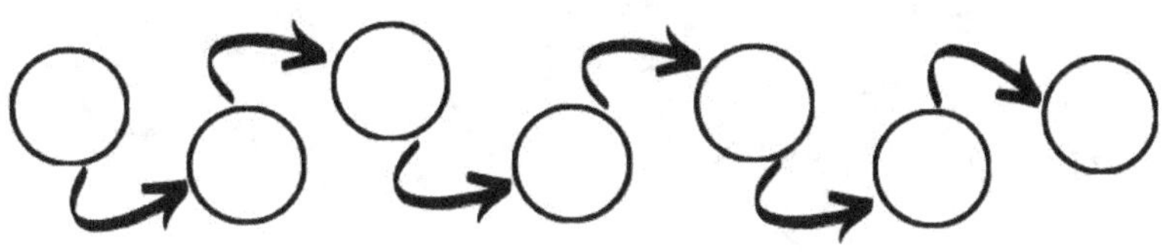

10-14-13-16-19-11-17

2-1-7-5-9-3-4

29-25-26-24-22-27-21

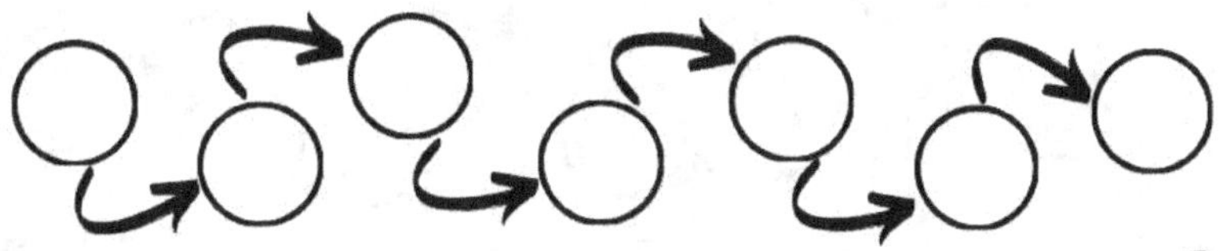

ADDITIONS

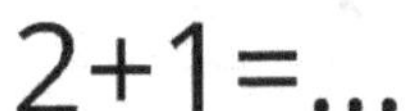

2+1=... 2+4=...

2+2=... 2+5=...

2+3=... 2+6=...

ARRANGE THE NUMBERS FROM THE SMALLEST TO THE LARGEST

21-26-25-24-28-29-27

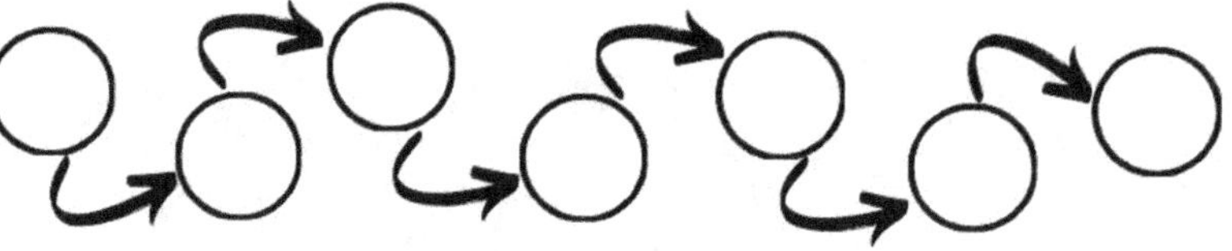

39-30-37-32-34-36-31

41-40-46-44-47-49-42

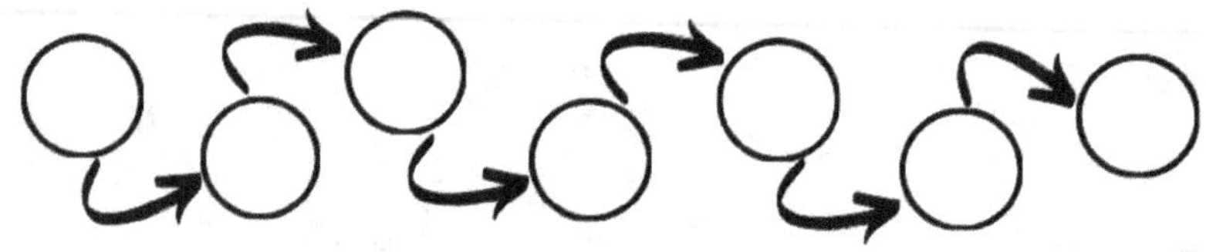

ADDITIONS

4+1=...   4+4=...

4+2=...   4+5=...

4+3=...   4+6=...

ARRANGE THE NUMBERS FROM THE SMALLEST TO THE LARGEST

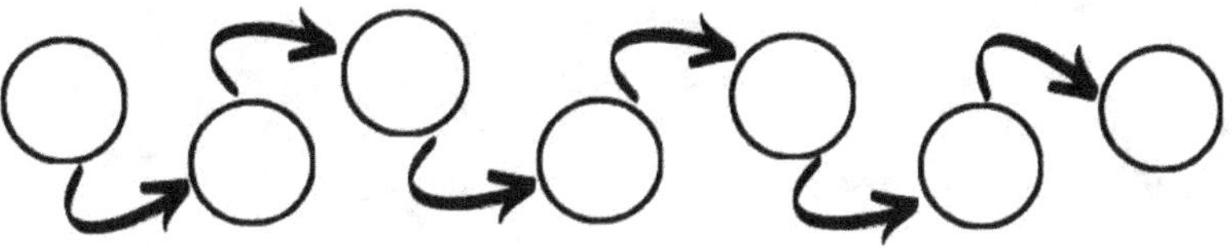

30-38-34-31-36-35-32

48-42-43-49-47-40-44

57-50-51-56-58-54-53

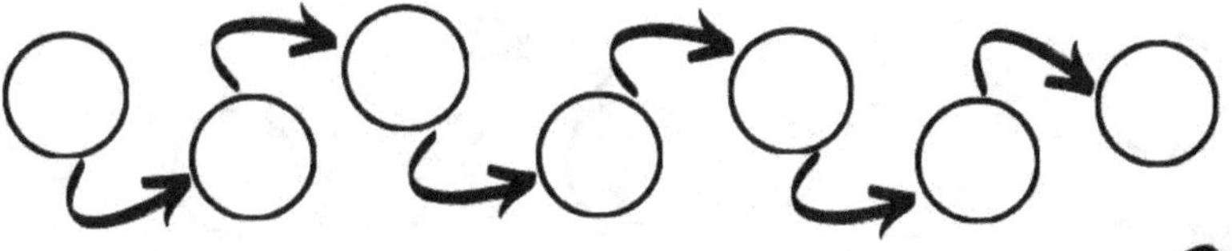

ADDITIONS

5+1=... 5+4=...

5+2=... 5+5=...

5+3=... 5+6=...

ARRANGE THE NUMBERS FROM THE SMALLEST TO THE LARGEST

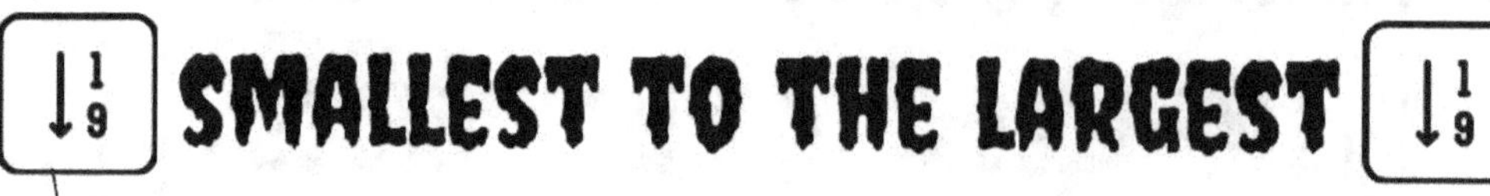

9-4-2-6-7-1-0

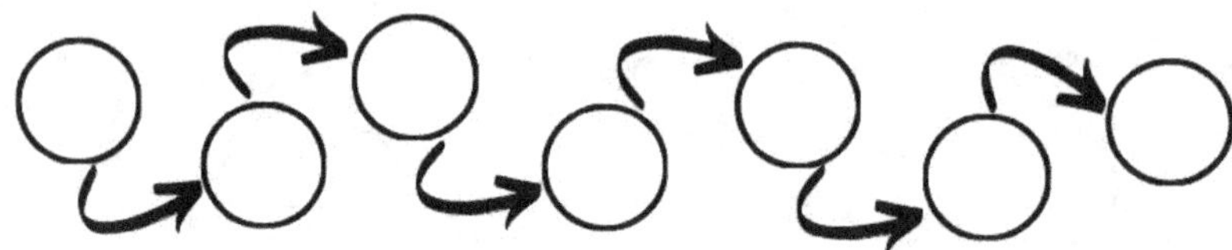

10-19-14-16-11-13-17

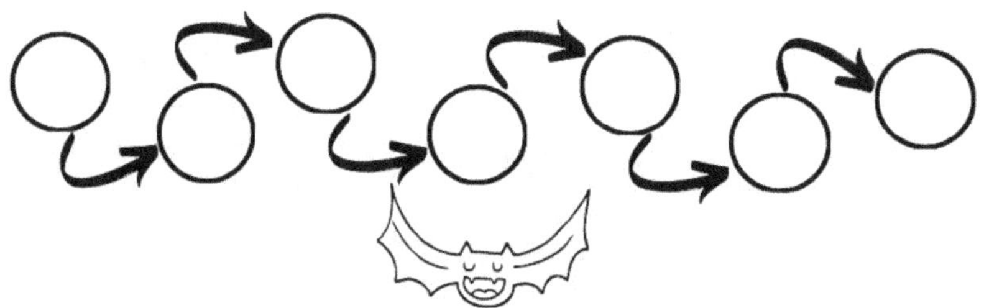

30-32-38-37-39-34-36

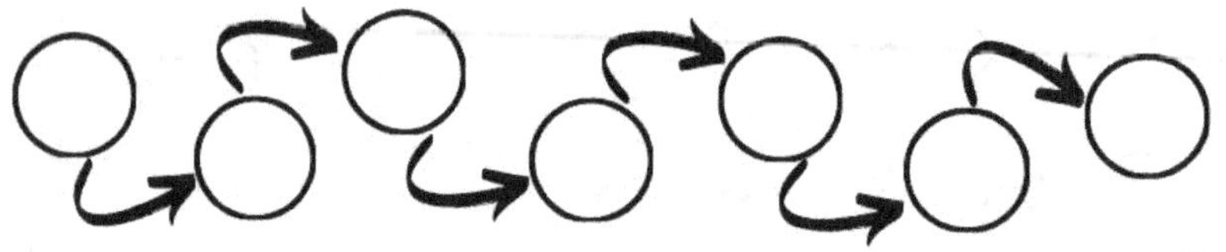

ADDITIONS

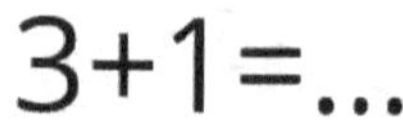

3+1=...	3+4=...
3+2=...	3+5=...
3+3=...	3+6=...

CONGRATULATIONS!
THIS CERTIFICATE OF GRADUATION
GRADUATED
1
THE BEST